UNKNOWN AMERICA

UNKNOWN AMERICA

Myths and little known oddities about
the greatest nation on earth

Michael P. Hart

ISBN-13: 9780692827802
ISBN-10: 0692827803
Library of Congress Control Number: 2017901546
Hart of America Productions,Birmingham,ALABAMA

Dedication

Many people, both living and dead, inspired me to write this book.

But none more so than my children

Victoria Grace, Mathew Patrick, and Lily Anastasia

Who I hope will always remember the importance of preserving, honoring and retelling the past accurately lest we forget the lessons it leaves behind

And to the love of my life, Tracy Renee, who inspires me every day with her wit, beauty, caring, grace and charm, and who pushes me to reach for heights I myself could not see.

Without her love and support this book would never be.

To each of them I dedicate this book

Table of Contents

Introduction

I n the book "THE LIFE OF REASON" Philosopher, writer and essayist George Santayana, famously penned the words: "Those who cannot remember the past are condemned to repeat it."

What Santayana was referring to is the failures that occur when people do not learn from their past mistakes and continue in their misguided ways; and in a larger sense the tragedies that can occur when humanity fails to learn, buries the truth of past mistakes or atrocities or worse, simply forgets.

Over the last several centuries, whether through human error, false reporting or simply neglect, history has often been a victim of forgetfulness or in far to many cases, revision.

While this book is chock full of historical trivia that many people have either forgotten, never knew, or were ever taught, it also serves to set the record straight on some of the inaccuracies and myths that have persisted throughout the history of this nation.

In this book you will learn about the private lives of some of the most famous Americans that shaped this nation as well as people you may never have heard of that the history books either ignored or whose stories were simply forgotten or altered.

In Unknown America, you will also learn fascinating facts, not just about the people that shaped America, but about the American culture and even about some of the little known oddities about the American experience.

While this book is far from comprehensive, hopefully it will inspire you to do your own research on the commonly held beliefs and teachings too many people passively accept as truth.

Simply stated; there's a lot of history in the past and unfortunately too much of it ignored, revised or deemed not worthy of being taught.

So be prepared to be amazed while you learn about some of the most fascinating people, places, plans and peculiarities that make up the "Unknown America"

Unknown States

Offbeat factoids and oddities about the states

ALABAMA

Weird AL: Alabama is the only state where sex toys are illegal. You need a Doctors prescription or risk facing serious penalties (Note: This law has been involved in several legal challenges and some stores do exist and are fighting to stay open)

* Alabama introduced the Mardi Gras to the western world. The celebration is held on Shrove Tuesday, the day before Lent begins in Mobile, a port city on the Alabama coast.

* Alabama workers built the first rocket that put humans on the moon. Actually Alabamians can rightfully claim the US Space program was started in their state when in 1950 Dr. Wernher von Braun arrived in the then tiny town of Huntsville. Von Braun lead The Marshall Space Flight Center, formerly part of the US Army, but now under NASA, which is the U.S. government's civilian rocketry and spacecraft propulsion research center. (rocketcenter.com)

* The world's first Electric Trolley System was introduced in Montgomery in 1886.

* Montgomery is the capital and the birthplace of the Confederate States of America and the Confederate flag was designed and first flown in Alabama in 1861. Jefferson Davis, the President of the Confederacy took the oath of office on the outside steps of the Alabama Statehouse.

* In 1902 Dr. Luther Leonidas Hill performed the first operation on a heart in the Western Hemisphere when he sutured a stab wound in a young boy's heart.
    The surgery occurred in Montgomery.

* Alabama can boast the first woman with disabilities to serve as Miss America. Heather Whitestone, who is deaf, was crowned in 1995.

* Adolph Hitler's typewriter survived from his mountain retreat and is exhibited at the history museum in Bessemer Alabama just Southwest of Birmingham

ALASKA

Weird AK: If Manhattan were as sparsely populated as Alaska there would be 28 people on the entire island.

* Outsiders first discovered Alaska in 1741 when Danish explorer Vitus Jonassen Bering sighted it on a voyage from Siberia.

* In 1867 United States Secretary of State William H. Seward offered Russia $7,200,000, or two cents per acre, for Alaska. On October 18, 1867 Alaska officially became the property of the United States. The Alaska Purchase would go on to be called "Seward's Folly"

* The state of Rhode Island could fit into Alaska 425 times and the state's coastline extends over 6,600 miles.

* Agattu, Attu, and Kiska part of a group of the Aleutian Islands of Alaska were we're the only parts of North America that were occupied by Japanese troops during World War II. The Japanese seizure of the Islands was strategically unimportant, but the islands did provide the Japanese with a base for raiding Alaska and limiting air and sea operations in the North Pacific. (worldwar2history.com)

ARIZONA

Weird AZ: There is a volcano in Arizona that goes by the name "Shit Pot Crater" because it "resembles" an "Accident" More weird: It's illegal for donkeys to sleep in bathtubs in Arizona

* Arizona observes Mountain Standard Time on a year round basis. The one exception is the Navajo Nation, located in the northeast corner of the state, which observes the daylight savings time change.

* The original London Bridge that formerly spanned the Thames River was dismantled in 1967 and shipped stone-by-stone and reconstructed in Lake Havasu City.

* Arizona, among all the states, has the largest percentage of its land set aside and designated as Indian lands.

* Arizona is home of several real ghost towns including: Tombstone, Ruby, Gillette, and Gunsight. The legendary 1881 Gunfight at the O.K. Corral in the Arizona Territory town of Tombstone is considered the most famous shootout in the American Old West, and lasted only 30 seconds. (It also didn't actually happen in the corral but between two nearby buildings).

* Arizona's most famous criminal, Ernesto Miranda, is the man responsible for mandated Miranda laws ("You have the right...").

ARKANSAS

Weird AR: Although no longer enforced, it is still technically illegal to mispronounce Arkansas, while in Arkansas.

* It is illegal for the Arkansas River, which separates Little Rock from North Little Rock, to rise above the Main Street Bridge.

* In Fayetteville it is illegal to kill any living creature.

* Voters in the Razorback state are only allowed five minutes to mark an election ballot.

CALIFORNIA

Weird CA: California's official state animal is the California Grizzly Bear. Which in a twist of irony was hunted to extinction, by Californians!

* Dick and Maurice McDonald opened the first McDonald's restaurant in San Bernardino, California in 1948, after another restaurant venture, a BBQ joint, had failed.

* The most corrupt politician in Fresno County history, Joseph Spinney was mayor for only ten minutes. In 1893, Spinney, sat on the Fresno board

of trustees. He was an enormously corrupt and had gained influence by representing the vice interests of the town. He also held a powerful swing vote that he used to push through political appointments. Spinney was made chairman of the board, effectively making him the mayor of the city...a position he held for a full ten minutes before resigning and nominating pal C.J. Craycroft to take his place. Apparently his tenure was just long enough to accomplish his intended goal – expanding and consolidating his power base. (Obnug.com)

* There is a palm tree and pine tree planted next to each other at the midpoint of California. The palm tree signifies the entrance to Southern California, while the pine tree signifies the entrance to Northern California

* The movie industry is based in Hollywood because movie makers were trying to get away from Thomas Edison (based in New Jersey). He had patents covering virtually the entire movie making process, but the Ninth Circuit Court of Appeals in California was known to rule against patent claims.

COLORADO
Weird CO: Colorado had to change 420 mile signs to 419.99 to keep people from stealing them. 420 is an urban reference to smoking marijuana.

* Colorado is the only state to turn down hosting the Olympics. Denver originally won the bid for the 1976 Winter Olympics, but the state's voters later rejected it due to infrastructure costs and environmental concerns. Innsbruck, Austria, hosted the 76 Winter Olympics

* The US Federal government owns more than 1/3 of Colorado's land.

* The 13th step of the state capital building in Denver is exactly 1 mile high above sea level.

* The chicken that lived without a head. On 10 September 1945 Lloyd Olsen and his wife Clara were killing chickens on their farm in Fruita,

Colorado. However one of the birds that went under Olsen's hatchet refused to die.

According to Olsen's Son-in-law "They got down to the end and had one who was still alive, up and walking around". The headless chicken kicked and ran, and didn't stop. It was placed in a box on the farm's screened porch for the night, and when Lloyd Olsen woke the following morning, "The damn thing was still alive," he exclaimed. As a matter of fact Mike, as the bird was named, lived, headless, for another 18 months! No, really!

(bbc.com)

* Colorado is the only state to have had three Governors serve in a single day. In 1904 an election between Democrat Alva Adams and the incumbent, Republican James H. Peabody, was full of corruption on both sides. The Democrats were accused of using "repeaters" in Denver and other places, while Republican mine owners forced mine laborers to vote Republican or lose their jobs. Based on the returns, Alva Adams was elected, but when Peabody found out about the voting fraud, he contested the election. But since Peabody's side had themselves engaged in fraudulent voting, an investigation was set forth. Adams took office but, following three months of deliberation, Adams was replaced by Peabody on March 16, 1905 on the condition that Peabody resign within 24 hours. Immediately following his resignation, Republican Lt. Gov. Jesse F. McDonald was sworn in as governor The result was that Colorado had three governors in one day.

(cospl.blogspot.com)

CONNECTICUT
Weird CT: In 1970 Connecticut refused to issue a man a drivers license on the basis his homosexuality made him dangerous to other drivers.

* "The Fundamental Orders" was the first constitution to be adopted by the American colonies in 1639. It established the structure and boundaries

of the newly formed government and ensured the rights of free men to elect their public officials—principles that were later embraced within the U.S. Constitution.

* War of 1812 Almost a Civil War
A month of meetings in 1814 to early 1815 were held in Hartford among federalists in New England who were considering secession from the U.S. and negotiating peace with Great Britain to end the War of 1812. The idea didn't receive much support, and Andrew Jackson's victory in the Battle of New Orleans soon made the issue moot. (Newsmax)

* In 1937, Connecticut became the first state to issue permanent license plates for cars.

* The USS Nautilus, the world's first nuclear submarine, was constructed in Groton, Connecticut, between 1952 and 1954. Much larger than its diesel-electric predecessors, it traveled at speeds in excess of 20 knots and could remain submerged almost indefinitely because its atomic engine required only a very small quantity of nuclear fuel and no air.

* In order for a pickle to be officially considered a pickle in the state, it must bounce. This law is presumably to keep local farmers from selling certain processed foods to maintain food safety and apparently "non bouncers" don't meet the states prescribed pH levels.

DELAWARE
Weird DE: There 25,000 headstones in the Delaware River left over from when the river was diverted over a graveyard. Every now and then one will wash up on shore.

* In 1787 in Dover, Delaware, the U.S. Constitution was unanimously ratified by all 30 delegates to the Delaware Constitutional Convention, making Delaware the first state of the modern United States.

* As a matter of fact Delaware was the first to fly the first "Betsy Ross" Flag in 1777 (Some historians doubt it was actually sewn by Ross since there were many "Flag Seamstresses" during that period. More on this later). Although the US declared its Independence from England in 1776, The United States of America, didn't become "Official' until the Constitution was ratified 11 years later.

* When conflict between the north and south broke out Delaware, which borders the Mason Dixon line, choose to remained in the Union. This was made evident when the Governor said that his state was the first to join the Union by ratifying the constitution, and would be the last to leave it.

* Delaware is the only state that does not have have a national park.

* In 1880, the first beauty contest in the United States was held in Rehoboth Beach. Thomas Edison was one of the judges. The "Miss United States" contest is considered the forerunner of the Miss America pageant.

FLORIDA
Weird FL: Florida has the highest rate of public masturbation in the U.S.
(Not sure how this was determined and we're not sure we want to know).

* The area code (321) 3… 2… 1… was assigned to Cape Canaveral in Florida to honor the space program. The area code, which is assigned to Brevard County, has been in use since November 1, 1999; it was assigned to Florida (instead of suburban Chicago) after a petition led by local resident to commemorate the NASA Space Programs impact on the County.

* On April 23, 1982 The Mayor of Key West declared the city would secede from the United States and the Conch Republic was born. The event was a tongue in cheek protest that was based on some very real concerns to the locals. The creation of the micro nation of the Conch Republic was

originally motivated by a U.S. Border Patrol roadblock and checkpoint that greatly inconvenienced residents and tourists. The Republic celebrates its "Independence Day" every April 23 as part of a week-long festival involving numerous businesses in Key West.

* The first Thanksgiving to occur in the Americas was in Florida, not Plymouth Rock. More than a half-century before the Pilgrims broke bread with the Wampanoags, Spanish colonists landing in St. Augustine, feasted with indigenous Timucua tribesmen in what some historians contend was America's real first Thanksgiving and not the one held 56 years later by the Pilgrims and Wampanoags in Plymouth, Massachusetts.
(History Channel)

* In 1964, during their first American tour, The Beatles refused to play a concert in Jacksonville until the audience was desegregated.
(Crazyfacts.com)

GEORGIA
Weird GA: Atlanta is the home of Coca Cola. In 1998 a Georgia student was suspended for wearing a Pepsi shirt on state Coke Day!

* The state of Georgia was in constant conflict with the Confederacy during the Civil War. The friction being caused mainly by Confederate President Jefferson Davis' desire to employ Georgia troops in the general war effort and the desire of Georgia Governor Joe Brown to retain the troops solely for the protection of his own state. The tension at one point growing to the point that Brown threatened to secede from the Confederacy.

* Muhammad Ali first fight under his new name after changing it from Cassius Clay, was against Jerry Quarry in Atlanta in 1970. Ali won in three rounds.

* The University of Georgia was the first public university in the United States. It received a charter from the state in 1785. Two other schools,

William & Mary and the University of North Carolina, also make this claim but by using different criteria (So we give the nod to UGA).

* Dahlonega was the site of the first gold rush in the nation during the late 1820s. The town even had a U.S. mint that produced gold coins with the "D" mark until 1861. Tourists can still pan for gold in this quaint Southern Town.

* Franklin Roosevelt died in Georgia while posing for a portrait at his Warm Springs retreat. He was in the living room with his long time mistress, Lucy Mercer, while the portrait was painted. According to biographer Doris Kearns Goodwin, it was about 1 p.m. that the president suddenly complained of a terrific pain in the back of his head and collapsed. One of the women summoned a doctor, who immediately recognized the symptoms of a massive cerebral hemorrhage. The unfinished portrait can still be seen at the "Little White House" in Warm Springs.

* Atlanta's Techwood Homes was The first public housing project in the U.S. It opened in 1935 and it was actually FDR that gave the dedication speech. The project housed only white residents until 1968. (Delano loved him some Georgia).

* The town of Madison escaped General William Sherman's destructive March to the Sea, but not because he found it "too beautiful to burn" as the myth goes. Sherman decided to spare Madison because a pro-Union senator named Joshua Hill, a fellow West Point grad, had a home there.

HAWII
Weird HI: It's illegal to own a Hamster or Hummingbird in Hawaii. Both would have devastating effects on local plants if they escaped.

* No matter how old you are or how long you've lived in the state, only people with Hawaiian ancestry are called "Hawaiians." People of non-Hawaiian ancestry—even those born and raised there—call themselves "locals."

* Hawaii was first settled by Polynesians sailing from other Pacific islands between 300 and 600 AD, Hawaii was visited in 1778 by British captain James Cook, who called the group the Sandwich Islands in honor of the Earl of Sandwich.

* Because of its continuous volcanic eruptions, Hawaii is the only state in the nation to have an increasing land area.

* In the 1960s, NASA astronauts trained for moon voyages by walking on Mauna Loa's hardened lava fields, which resemble the surface of the moon.

* In the early 1800's Early missionaries were shocked to find that Hawaiian mothers practiced infanticide if the babies were deformed or diseased or if there were already too many children. They were also shocked by the extreme displays of grief (such as knocking out their own teeth or tattooing their own tongues) after the death of a loved one.

* Hawaii is 2,390 miles away from the nearest continent (North America) and is considered the most isolated population center on earth.
    (Random History)

IDAHO
Weird ID: At the stroke of midnight on New Years Idaho drops a giant Potato rather than a ball.

* The capital city of Boise was named when French-Canadian trappers arrived in the early 1800s and were so relieved to see the forest and river that they exclaimed "Les bois! Les bois!" which translates; "The trees"

* In Pocatello, it's against the law to be seen in person without a smile on your face.

* Idaho's state seal is the only one in the U.S. designed by a woman. In 1890, Emma Edwards Green submitted the design for the State Seal competition

sponsored by the First state Legislature. Grenn won and was awarded $100 by Governor N. B. Willey for her design of the state Great Seal, which depicts a miner, a woman and various natural resources of Idaho.

ILLINOIS

Weird IL: The 4th Illinois Infantry stole General Santa Anna of Mexico, prosthetic leg during the Mexican - American War. And to this day the state refuses to give it back.

* Illinois, the birthplace of Abraham Lincoln, who signed the Emancipation Proclamation into law, was the first State to abolish slavery.

* Aurora is known as the City of Lights because it was the first US city to use electric street lighting throughout the entire city.

* The first public office that Abraham Lincoln took was as postmaster in New Salem.

* Chicago's nickname, the Windy City, has nothing to do with meteorology. The epithet—from a New York City journalist—actually referred to the long-winded politicians campaigning for the World's Columbian Exhibition of 1893.

INDIANA

Weird IN: In 1897 the state legislature tried to round pi, an immutable law of mathematics, up from it's 1 million decimal places to simply 3.2.

* Baseball was practically born in Indiana – Fort Wayne, to be exact. The very first professional game had occurred in the town on May 4, 1871.

* If it wasn't for Indiana, New York's Empire State Building, Rockefeller Center, the Pentagon, the U.S. Treasury, and many other buildings in Washington D.C. would never exist. 14 state capitols would never be

erected either, all because Indiana's home to a sea of limestone deep below the earth. It happens to have one of the richest deposits of that type of stone found anywhere on the planet.

* On October 6, 1866, a gang by the name of the "Reno Brothers" thought it a good idea to rob a train. They did it in Jackson County in Indiana, making off with a hefty $13,000. It was the first train robbery ever in history.
   -Movoto

IOWA
Weird IA: The last prisoner to be executed in Iowa requested a single olive for his last meal, hoping an olive tree would spring from his body as a sign of peace.

* A surveying mistake almost caused a war between Iowa and Missouri in the 1830s. The surveyor's state boundary line slanted four miles further north on the east side than the west because he forgot to adjust his compass. Another official was sent to resurvey, but his line was a bit north of the original line, to the tune of 2,600 acres. When a Missouri official tried to collect taxes from the settlers who lived in the disputed acres, an Iowa sheriff arrested him. The governors of each state threatened each other with combat, with militias and volunteers called to gather at the border. Before any shots were fired, the federal government stepped in and drew the line, literally.

* When the Civil War broke out, Iowa had only been a state for 15 years and had a population of just 600,000. Though only 76,534 Iowa men served in the Union army no other state had a higher percentage of its male population serve. Iowa even had a regiment called the "Greybeards" because the men were all elderly, including one octogenarian.

KANSAS
Weird KS: In 2008 a tornado hit Kansas State University. It destroyed only one building; The Wind Erosion Lab.

* After the Kansas-Nebraska Act of 1854 opened the two territories to settlement and allowed the new settlers to decide whether the states would be admitted to the union as "free" or "slave", North and South competed to send the most settlers into the region. This quickly led to violence and the territory became known as "Bleeding Kansas."

* Meade's Ranch in Osborne County, Kansas, is the Geodetic Center of North America—the point of reference by which all property lines and boundaries in North America are surveyed.

KENTUCKY

Weird KY: In 1876 it mysteriously rained over a cloudless Kentucky town. It was believed a massive flock of Buzzards had exploded over the town after gorging themselves on dead horses.

* Kentucky was originally a part of Virginia, but that arrangement didn't work out too well for early Kentuckians. Since the interests of Kentucky's residents didn't always align with those of Virginians. On June 1, 1792, Virginia gave Kentucky permission to break off on its own to become the 15th state.

* Thomas Edison made the first major public display of his newly created incandescent light bulb at Louisville's Southern Exposition in 1883. Edison had actually lived in Louisville in the mid-1860s working as a Western Union telegraph operator. Supposedly he was fired after spilling a jar of acid while doing an experiment on company time.

LOUISIANA

Weird LA: Louisiana is the prison capital of the world; 1 out of every 86 people are in the clink.

* Louisiana is the only state in the US that is not divided into counties. Rather these divisions are defined as "parishes." A nod to the early churches that dotted the landscape while to region was under the rule of France and Spain.

* In 1861, Louisiana seceded from the union but did not immediately join the Confederate States of America. The state remained independent for two months prior to joining the Confederacy and flew a pelican flag in place of an American flag. Seven years later, in 1868, Louisiana rejoined the United States.

MAINE
Weird ME: Cabot Cove Maine, the setting for "Murder She Wrote", has 50% more murders than Honduras, the murder capital of the world.

* With a total area of 33,215 square miles the state covers nearly as many square miles as the other five New England states combined.

* In 1641, York was America's first chartered city. It then became the nation's first incorporated city in 1642. Maine is the only American state with a one-syllable name.

* The first Revolutionary War naval battle was fought in Buzzards Bay, near Fairhaven in 1775.

MARYLAND
Weird MD: If you own a toilet in Maryland, you pay a $60.00 per year tax for flushing it. The Chesapeake Bay Restoration Fee, known as the flush tax, generates millions of dollars to help restore the Chesapeake Bay.

* On the morning of August 10, 1813 residents of Saint Michaels, were warned of a British attack and hoisted lanterns to the masts of ships and in the tops of the trees. The height of the light caused the British to overshoot the town—and this was the first known blackout.

* As one of the most distinctive state flags in the union, the Maryland State flag is the only state flag to be based on English heraldry. The black and gold design on the quartered flag is based on the coat of arms of the Calvert family.

* The John Hopkins School of Medicine in Baltimore employed the first female professor of medicine in 1901.

MASSACHUSETTS
Weird MA: There is a state law that forbids snoring unless all of your doors and windows are locked.

* The first public school system was founded in Boston in 1635 and Boston Latin was our country's first public school. The Mather School in Dorchester was founded in 1639 as the first public elementary school.

* The first flag of the United American Colonies was raised on Prospect Hill in Somerville, in 1776.

* The first subway system in the United States was built in Boston not NYC.

* When you take a stroll on the Boston Common, you are visiting the nation's first public park, established in 1634 and the first public beach, Revere Beach, is also located in Massachusetts.

MICHIGAN
Weird MI: One Michigan county lost 1.25 Million Dollars in 2007 to a Nigerian scammer who had contacted the county by email.

* Although the Treaty of Paris granted the Northwest Territories to the United States in 1783, most of the settlers and Native American Indians living in Detroit favored the British, who continued to maintain control. It wasn't until a coalition of Indian tribes, known as the Western Confederacy, lost the Battle of Fallen Timbers in 1795 that the British finally evacuated in 1796 and the new United States took control.

* The J.W. Westcott II, is a delivery boat which operates out of Detroit. It is the world's only floating post office. It delivers mail to crews on vessels transiting the Detroit River. Mail is delivered by being addressed "*Vessel Name,*

Marine Post Office, Detroit, Michigan, 48222." The Zip code 48222 is exclusive to the floating post office.

* Detroit residents were the first in the nation to have phone numbers. It seems that by 1879, the city had grown so large that operators were no longer able to route the calls by name alone.

MINNESOTA
Weird MN: Sinclair Lewis wrote a satirical novel entitled "Main Street" which criticized the closed mindedness of a fictional town in Minnesota. It was banned by the town of Alexandria because they disagreed with it. More or less proving Lewis' point.

* Minnesota is the only state to have an official state photograph.

* On December 26, 1862, 38 of 303 convicted Dakota Indians were hanged in Mankato in the largest mass execution in American history. Frustrated by the U.S. government's failure to make treaty payments on time and supply their families with food as promised, a group of warriors killed several settlers, igniting a conflict that lasted four months. Although President Abraham Lincoln commuted the death sentences of 264 convicted Dakota, Congress passed a law expelling all Dakota bands from Minnesota a few months later.

* The first successful open heart surgery was performed on a 5-year-old girl on September 2, 1952, by Dr. Floyd John Lewis and Dr. Clarence Walton Lillehei at the University of Minnesota. With her body temperature reduced to 81 degrees Fahrenheit, the girl was able to survive for 10 minutes while the doctors repaired a congenital hole in her heart. (This operation was different than the one performed in Alabama 50 years earlier as it was for a heart defect and not a wound).

MISSISSIPPI
Weird MS: In 1970 Mississippi, banned Sesame Street because it featured a racially integrated cast of children.

* The Musical Genre' "The Blues" originated in the Mississippi Delta after the Civil War. Rooted in the songs sung by slaves working in the fields and African spirituals, the Blues offered an escape from oppression and a means of expression for many African Americans.

* While on a hunting expedition with Mississippi Governor Andrew Longino in November of 1902, President Theodore Roosevelt refused to shoot a bear that had been captured and tied to a tree. Afterward, a satirical cartoon of the event was published, inspiring a Brooklyn candy shop owner to create a stuffed "Teddy's" Bear.

* Mississippi is the only state in which over two thirds of its residents are classified as either overweight or obese.

MISSOURI
Weird MO: Yellow Margarine is Illegal in Mizzou. Contraband dealers could face six months in jail and a $500 fine.

* On Oct. 27, 1838, after Mormons attacked a militia believed to be an anti-Mormon mob, Governor Lilburn Boggs issued an "Extermination Order," which directed General John Clark to treat all members of the Mormon Church as enemies that must either be exterminated or removed from the state of Missouri. Governor Christopher Bond officially rescinded the order in 1976.

* During the Civil War, Missourians were split in their allegiances, supplying both Union and Confederate forces with troops.

* In 1873, Susan Elizabeth Blow opened the first public kindergarten in the United States in St. Louis after having learning of the kindergarten methods of philosopher Friedrich Froebel while traveling in Germany years earlier.

* Missouri is the only state that still has its own schools for severely disabled students.

MONTANA

Weird MT: The Miley Cyrus Character, Hannah Montana was almost called Alexis Texas.

* Montana is home to the Triple Divide, the hydrological apex of North America on Triple Divide Peak. From this spot, water flows to three oceans: Hudson Bay(Arctic), Gulf of Mexico (Atlantic), and the Pacific Ocean.

* Montana is is the only state in the United States whose constitution recognizes the cultural heritage of the American Indians and is committed to the preservation of their cultural integrity.

* Montana is the only state in the United States without a modern naval ship named in its honor.

* For many years, Montana was the only state with no daytime speed limit.

NEBRASKA

Weird NE: The state drink of the Cornhusker state is Kool-aid.

* Nebraska is the only state with a non-partisan, unicameral legislature. Thought to be more efficient, cost-effective and able to eliminate secretive conference committee meetings common in bicameral legislatures, Nebraska has been governing by a single-house legislature since 1937.

* The only roller skating museum in the world is located in Lincoln.

NEVADA

Weird NV: John Wayne and 90 other people, involved in the 1955 film "The Conqueror" are believed to have contracted Cancer from "A" bomb tests that were occurring upwind of them in Nevada.

* In 1864, in an effort to hasten its admission to the union, Nevada's entire state constitution was sent to Washington, D.C., by telegram.

* Nevada was the first state to ratify the 15th Amendment to the U.S. Constitution, which gave African-American men the right to vote, on March 1, 1869.

Roughly 85% of Nevada is actually owned by the US Government.

NEW HAMPSHIRE
Weird NH: The slogan on New Hampshire license plates is "Live free or Die"... The plates are made by convicts in state Prisons.

* New Hampshire, one of the original 13 colonies, was the first state to have its own state constitution.

* New Hampshire is the only state to have hosted the formal conclusion of a foreign war. In 1905, the treaty ending the Russo-Japanese War was signed in Portsmouth.

* New Hampshire adopted the first legal lottery in the U.S. in 1963.

NEW JERSEY
Weird NJ: New Jersey once tried to use Eminent Domain on an elderly woman's home and transfer it to Donald Trump so that he could build a limousine parking lot on the property.

* One of the original 13 colonies, New Jersey was named for the island of Jersey in the English Channel.

* New Jersey was the site of more than 100 battles during the fight for American independence, garnering it the nickname; The "Crossroads of the Revolution".

* New Jersey is the only state in the Union that requires a code of humane standards for farm animals.

NEW MEXICO

Weird NM: New Mexico's first graduating class was in 1893 and had only 1 student. He was shot and killed before graduating.

* Santa Fe was founded 10 years before the Pilgrims landed at Plymouth.

The Spanish were in New Mexico long before the Mayflower landed on Massachusett's Plymouth rock. Santa Fe is not only the oldest European city west of the Mississippi River; it's the oldest capital city in North America, dating to 1610.

*The New Mexico Constitution officially bars "idiots" from voting. Originally the term "idiot" referred to those suffering some sort of mental illness. Since the usage of the word idiot has changed over the years it is merely an outdated law but a rather amusing one.

NEW YORK

Weird NY: In 1922 New Yorkers rioted over whether it was OK or not to wear a straw hat past the "Socially Acceptable" date of September 15th. The riot lasted over 8 days... Although many arrests were made, no straw hats were injured.

* The Dutch first settled along the Hudson River in 1624; two years later they established the colony of New Amsterdam (The first name of New York City) on Manhattan Island. In 1664, the English took control of the area and renamed it New York.

* New York City was the first capital of the United States after the Constitution was ratified in 1788. On April 30, 1789, George Washington was inaugurated as the nation's first president at Federal Hall, located on Wall Street.

* The popular and often provocative tabloid New York Post was originally established by Alexander Hamilton in 1801 as a Federalist newspaper

called the New York Evening Post. Hamilton was one of the author of the Federalist papers (Which help "Sell" the colonies on ratification of the Constitution) and the nation's first secretary of the treasury.

NORTH CAROLINA

Weird NC: In 1961 the US Air Force accidentally dropped two Nuclear Bombs on North Carolina. Both with 250 times the destructive power than the one dropped on Hiroshima.

* One of the original 13 colonies, North Carolina was the first state to instruct its delegates to vote for independence from the British crown during the Continental Congress.

* The first child born in America of English descent was in NC. A girl named Virginia Dare was born on August 18, 1587. Virginia was one of the members of the "Lost Colony," which was a late 16th-century attempt by Queen Elizabeth I to establish a permanent English settlement in the region.

NORTH DAKOTA

Weird ND: Because of an error in the states 1889 Constitution, North Dakota was not legally a state until 2011.

* The geographical center of North America—marked by a 21-foot monument constructed out of stones—lies in the town of Rugby, North Dakota.

* There was an intense rivalry between North and South Dakota prior to becoming states over which one would be admitted to the union first. When the time came for their formal admission, President Benjamin Harrison randomly selected which bill to sign first, and he purposely did not record the order in which the bills were signed presumably to ease some of the friction between the two states.

OHIO

Weird OH: The Cuyahoga River that goes through Cleveland is so polluted that is has caught fire at least 15 times.

* First colonized by French fur traders, Ohio became a British possession following the French and Indian War in 1754. At the end of the American Revolution, Britain ceded control of the territory to the newly formed United States and it became part of the Northwest Territory.

* The "Mother of Modern Presidents," Ohio was the birthplace of seven U.S. presidents: Ulysses S. Grant, Rutherford B. Hayes, James Garfield, Benjamin Harrison, William McKinley, William H. Taft and Warren G. Harding.

OKLAHOMA

Weird OK: Oklahoma's state vegetable is the Watermelon, which is a fruit.

* Oklahoma became the very last state to make Christmas legal after again in 1907 after a 200 year ban that originated in England, despite the US making it a federal holiday in 1870.

* In 1905, representatives from the Cherokee, Seminole, Creek, Choctaw and Chickasaw nations—known as the Five Civilized Tribes—submitted a constitution for a separate Indian state to be called Sequoyah. The US Congress refused to consider the request for statehood and on November 16, 1907, Indian and Oklahoma territories were combined to form present day Oklahoma.

OREGON

Weird OR: The smallest urban park in the world is a 2 foot circle in Portland. Milk Ends Park is just big enough for a single plant.

* Following exploration by the Spanish and French, in the 17th and 18th centuries, Oregon was mapped by the Lewis and Clark expedition in

their search for the Northwest Passage. Oregon's Crater Lake, formed in the remnant of an ancient volcano, is the deepest lake in the United States.

* Until about 1884, the Oregon Trail was the most heavily traveled and the most used of all routes in the westward expansion of the United States.

PENNSYLVANIA

Weird PA: In Pennsylvania it is illegal to use milk crates for anything but milk. Unauthorized use can result in a $300.00 fine and up to 90 days in jail.

* Pennsylvania's capital, Philadelphia, was the site of the first and second Continental Congresses in 1774 and 1775, the latter produced the Declaration of Independence, which sparked the American Revolution.

* Philadelphia was the nation's capital from 1790 until a permanent capital was established in Washington, D.C. in 1800.

* In 1903, the Boston Americans and Pittsburgh Pirates played each other in the first official World Series.

RHODE ISLAND

Weird RI: The mascot of the Rhode Island School of Design in named "Scrotie". The Basketball team, the Balls, and the Hockey team is the Nads... Now that's really weird!

* Rhode Island which happen to be the smallest US State happens to have the longest name. Officially "The State of Rhode Island and Providence Plantations".

* Rhode Island was founded by Roger Williams in 1636, who was banished from the Massachusetts colony for advocating for religious tolerance and the separation of church and state.

SOUTH CAROLINA

Weird SC: Its against the law in this Southern state for anyone under the age of 18 to play pinball.

* South Carolina was the first state to have a golf course. On September 29, 1786, the South Carolina Golf Club was formed and the nations first course was built after having imported balls and clubs from Scotland years before.

* On November 2, 1954, Strom Thurmond a former Governor, became the first person to be elected to the U.S. Senate as a write-in candidate, winning 63 percent of the vote.

SOUTH DAKOTA

Weird SD: The Pine Ridge Indian Reservation has one of the lowest standards of living anywhere in the world. Life expectancy is only 48 years. Its only lower in Haiti.

* The original design for Mount Rushmore included Presidents George Washington, Thomas Jefferson, Abraham Lincoln and Theodore Roosevelt from head to waist, but Sculptor Gutzon Borglum, died before the work was completed and Congress cut off funding as the nation became faced with World War I.

TENNESSEE

Weird TN: The electric chair in the Volunteer state is constructed from the Gallows it replaced in 1916.

* Memphis was founded in May of 1819 by John Overton and James Winchester, along with a future President of the United States, Andrew Jackson.

* The architect of the Tennessee State Capitol in Nashville, William Strickland, died during the building's construction. At his request, he was entombed within the structure's walls.

* Although Tennessee stretches 432 miles from east to west, its north and south boundries are only 112 miles apart.

TEXAS

Weird TX: Coal Plants in Texas produce as much pollution as the entire Country of Egypt. Which is home to 86 million people.

* According to the 1845 state constitution, Texas has the right, if it so desires, to subdivide into five smaller states.

* At one time or another, Texas has flown the flag of six separate nations: Spain, France, Mexico, the Republic of Texas, the Confederate States of America and the United States. This is where the original Six Flags amusement park, which opened in Arlington in 1961, derives it's name.

* In the 1850s, the U.S. War Department imported camels into Texas twice because they thought they'd come in handy for the Indian Wars.

* Texas is the only U.S. state that entered the Union by treaty rather than territorial annexation.

UTAH

Weird UT: A Teacher in Utah was fired for writing a blog post about Homophones. The Principal believed it would associate the school with Homosexuality.

* On May 10, 1869, the first transcontinental railroad was completed when the Union and Central Pacific joined at Promontory Summit in Utah Territory.

* Approximately 60% of the states residents are members of the Mormon Church.

VERMONT

Weird VT: The tallest building in the state is an 11 story Apartment Building. It is the shortest "Tallest Building" in any given state in the nation.

* During the American Revolution, Vermont declared independence separately from the original 13 colonies, although the Continental Congress refused to recognize it.

* Vermont was finally admitted to the union as the 14th state in 1790, after 14 years as an independent republic.

* On October 5, 1789, congressman Matthew Lyon was indicted under the Sedition Act for criticizing President John Adams in a letter he had written to Spooner's Vermont Journal. Although convicted and sentenced to four months in jail, Lyon was re-elected while incarcerated.

VIRGINIA

Weird VA: In 1966 a School Board in Hanover banned "To Kill a Mockingbird" for being "Immoral". The books Author, Harper Lee set up a fund to educate the school board as she believed them to be illiterate.

* On October 19, 1781, following three weeks of continuous bombardment, British General Lord Charles Cornwallis surrendered to George Washington in the Battle of Yorktown in Virginia, essentially bringing the American Revolution to an end.

* Virginia's borders have expanded and contracted numerous times since its inception. In 1792, nine counties known as the Kentucky District of Virginia entered the union as the state of Kentucky, and in 1863, western counties of Virginia were approved to enter the union as the state of West Virginia.

* The mansion that sits high atop Arlington National Cemetery was once the home of Confederate General Robert E. Lee who abandoned the home at the onset of war. In 1864 the estate was established as a national cemetery with the first interred there being Union Soldiers.

WASHINGTON

Weird WA: Washington did not officially ban sex with animals until 2005 when a man ruptured his colon at an animal brothel.

* Granted statehood in 1889, Washington; it is the only state named after a president.

* In an attempt to honor her father, a Civil War veteran who had raised six children by himself after his wife died in childbirth, Spokane resident Sonora Smart Dodd garnered support for the first statewide Father's Day celebration on June 19, 1910. Afterward, Dodd continued to press for a national observance; although the idea was backed by President Woodrow Wilson in 1916 and President Calvin Coolidge in 1924, Father's Day did not become a federal holiday until 1972.

WEST VIRGINIA

Weird WV: Huntington West Virginia, with a population of 50,000 has more pizza joints than the rest of the state has gyms.

* When the state of Virginia voted to secede from the United States during the Civil War the people of the western region of the state opposed the decision and organized to form their own state, West Virginia, in support of the Union. Congress granted statehood to West Virginia on June 20, 1863.

* The Greenbrier, a luxurious resort in the Allegheny Mountains was used at the outset of World War II to house diplomats from Germany, Italy and Japan until American diplomats detained overseas could be returned home safely in exchange.

* In 1942, West Virginia enacted a law that required students and teachers to salute the American flag and recite the Pledge of Allegiance. When Walter Barnette refused to do so on the grounds that it contradicted his religious beliefs, he was expelled from school. On June 14, 1943, the U.S. Supreme Court ruled in West Virginia State Board of Education v. Barnette that forcing individuals to salute the flag was a violation of their freedom of speech and religion.

WISCONSIN
Weird WI: The plastic Flamingo lawn ornament is the official bird of Madison, Wisconsin.

* Wisconsin earned the nickname "Badger State," because its earliest white inhabitants were itinerant lead miners who burrowed into the hills for shelter rather than waste time and resources on a more permanent structure.

* Enraged by the recent passage of the Kansas-Nebraska Act, Alvan Bovay convened a meeting at a schoolhouse to create a new political party that would defend against the expansion of slavery. It was during this meeting, on March 20, 1854, that the Republican Party was established.

WYOMING
Weird WY: (As of publication) There are only two Escalators in the entire state.

* Wyoming was the first U.S. state to allow women to vote. An achievement that represented one of the early victories of the American women's suffrage movement.

* Devils Tower, a natural rock formation resulting from a volcanic intrusion and a sacred site for many Plains Indians, was designated the first national monument in the U.S. by President Theodore Roosevelt on September 24, 1906.
(HISTORY.com)

2

Unknown Americans

Fascinating Americans that the history books mostly ignored or just got wrong

HartofAmerica.net

MAUDIE HOPKINS

Hopkins who died on August 17, 2008 was an American woman believed to be the last publicly known surviving widow of a Civil War veteran

Born in Baxter County, Arkansas, she married William M. Cantrell, who was 86 when they wed, on February 2, 1934, when she was 19. Cantrell had enlisted in the Confederate States Army at age 16 in Pikeville, Kentucky, and served in General Samuel G. French's Battalion of the Virginia Infantry.

It was not uncommon for young women in Arkansas to marry former Confederate soldiers mainly to receive their pensions upon their deaths However in 1937 the state passed a law that prevented these women from receiving these pensions.

CONCEPTION PICCIOTTO

Conception, known to many as "Connie" was a Spanish immigrant and was the primary guardian of the anti-nuclear-proliferation vigil stationed along Pennsylvania Avenue.

Ms. Picciotto spent more than 30 years of her life outside the White House "to stop the world from being destroyed."

Through her presence, and hand written signs, she said she hoped to remind others to take whatever action they could, to help end wars and stop violence, particularly against children.

A diminutive woman always clad in a helmet and headscarf, Picciotto was a curious and controversial figure in DC. Fellow activists lauded her as a heroine. Critics dismissed her as foolish, perhaps mentally unstable. Ms. Picciotto thought the US Government responsible for many of her physical ailments. She died on January 25 2016

-Washington Post

MYTH BUSTER ALERT!
CLAUDETTE COLVIN

Before there was Rosa Parks there was Claudette Colvin

Colvin is a pioneer of the African American Civil Rights. On March 2, 1955, Colvin was actually the first person arrested for resisting bus segregation, not Rosa Parks. by refusing to give up her bus seat in Montgomery Alabama

For many years, Montgomery's black leaders did not publicize Colvin's pioneering effort because, fearing the optic that in fact Colvin, who was just a 15 year old teenager at the time, was pregnant by a married man, and that fact might tarnish the movement, Rosa Parks was choosen instead. Words like "feisty", "mouthy", and "emotional" were used to describe Miss Colvin, while the older Parks was viewed as being calm, well-mannered, and studious. Because of the social norms of the time and her youth, the NAACP leaders worried about using her to symbolize their boycott.

ELIZABETH GRAHAM

And before there was Claudette Colvin, there was Elizabeth Jennings Graham

In the 1850s, horse-drawn street cars were a popular mode of transportation, especially in large cities like New York. These privately-owned vehicles could deny service to anyone for any reason. On Sunday, July 16, 1854, Graham was running late to church and boarded a street car. The conductor ordered her to get off, but she refused. Eventually, it took a police officer to remove her from the street car.

Graham's story inspired African American New Yorkers to stand up for their rights and fight against racial discrimination in public transportation. The story received national attention —especially when Elizabeth filed a lawsuit against the driver and the Third Avenue Railroad Company. Her lawyer, Chester A. Arthur, would later go on to be the president of the US.

In 1855, Graham won her case and the court declared that African American persons should have the same rights to access to the transit system. As a result The system in New York was desegregated by 1861, 100 years before Colvin and then Parks refused to give up their seats on a buses in Alabama.

-New York Times

MOLLY PITCHER

Although not her real name, Most sources identify the real Molly Pitcher as Mary Ludwig. Her first husband was William Hays. During the Revolutionary War, Hays was as a gunner in the Continental Army. It was common at the time for wives to be near their husbands in battle and help as needed.

June 28, 1778 was a brutally hot day in Freehold, New Jersey where Hays was fighting in the Battle of Monmouth. His wife was there as well, and she made countless trips to a nearby spring to fill pitchers of cold water for soldiers to drink and to pour over their cannons to cool them down.

As legend has it, the soldiers nicknamed her Molly Pitcher for her tireless efforts. When Pitcher's husband collapsed at his cannon position and was unable to continue with the fight. Molly dropped her water pitcher and took his place, manning the weapon throughout the remainder of the battle until the Colonists achieved victory. According to the National Archives, there was a documented witness to Pitcher's heroic acts, who reported a cannon shot passing through her legs on the battlefield, leaving her unscathed.

-Biography.com

JAMES GORDON BENNETT

As the founding publisher of The New York Herald, he invented the modern American newspaper. Bennett was Scottish-born American editor who shaped many of the methods of modern journalism.

With a capital investment of $500 Bennett published the first of a four-page Herald on May 6, 1835 from a cellar. He made the paper a great commercial success by devoting attention particularly to the gathering of news and was the first to introduce many of the methods of modern news reporting. He published the first Wall Street financial article to appear in any American newspaper; was the first, to establish correspondents in Europe; was the first, to obtain reports in full by telegraph of long political speeches. During the Civil War a he maintained a staff of 63 war correspondents; was a leader in the use of illustrations. It can be argued that James Bennett was the Godfather of the modern American Media

MARGARET HIGGINS SANGER

Sanger was an American birth control activist, sex educator, writer, and nurse. Sanger popularized the term "birth control", opened the first birth control clinic in the United States, and established organizations that evolved into the Planned Parenthood Federation of America. Sanger is also one of the most controversial figures on the American Landscape.

An entire book could be written on Sanger's controversial beliefs and activism. In February 1917, the first issue of Sanger's journal, *The Birth Control Review*, was published. She was *The Review*'s editor until 1929, and used her editorials to promote birth control and eugenics. For Sanger, these issues were inseparable.

The Positive eugenics movement promoted the idea of improving the human population by encouraging "fit" people to reproduce. Negative eugenics, conversely, attempted to "improve" the human population by discouraging "unfit" people from reproducing.

The "unfit" people included the poor, the sick, the disabled, and the "feeble-minded," the "idiots," the "morons," and the "insane." And "discouragement" from reproducing included the use of force. It has been reported that Sanger also believed that Negative Eugenics should be employed to control the Black population primarily in the inner cities.

One of Sanger's more memorable and troubling quotes was: "*The most merciful thing that a family does to one of its infant members is to kill it*".

ROSETTA THARPE

Sister Rosetta Tharpe was an American singer, songwriter, guitarist and recording artist Tharpe has been referred to by many as the Godmother of Rock and Roll.. A pioneer of mid-20th-century music, she attained popularity in the 1930s and 1940s with her Gospel recordings, characterized by a unique mixture of spiritual lyrics and rhythmic accompaniment that was a precursor of rock and roll. She was the first great recording star among the first gospel musicians to appeal to rhythm and blues and rock-and-roll audiences, later being referred to as "the original soul sister". Tharpe influenced early rock-and-roll musicians, including Little Richard, Johnny Cash, Chuck Berry, Elvis Presley and Jerry Lee Lewis.

FRANK WILLS

Wills was working as a security guard at the Watergate hotel in 1972 when he discovered tape propping a door open in the hotel and called the police. This discovery led to the Watergate scandal where GOP Operatives were found to have electronically bugged the Headquarters of the Democratic National Convention. The scandal that would eventually force President Nixon to resign. While the reason why is not totally clear, Wills lost his job shortly after the incident. He had difficulty finding work after the Watergate scandal, with one potential employer citing a fear of losing federal funding if they hired him. Wills lived the rest of his life in relative poverty and obscurity.

MYTH BUSTER ALERT!
BETSY ROSS

So you thought you knew this one... But not so fast!

One of American history's most persistent legends involves Betsy Ross, a Philadelphia seamstress who supposedly made the first American flag. As the story goes, in 1776 Ross was commissioned to sew the flag—which then featured a circle of 13 stars—by a small committee that included George Washington. Ross supposedly produced her famous flag a few days later and even changed the design to make the stars five-pointed rather than six-pointed.

While versions of this story continue to be taught in American classrooms, most historians dismiss it as a falsehood. Newspapers from the time make no reference to Ross or the meeting, and Washington never mentioned her involvement in creating the flag. In fact, the Ross legend didn't even make its first appearance until 1870, when her grandson, William Canby, related it to the Historical Society of Pennsylvania. But outside of showing affidavits from family members, no convincing evidence to support Canby's claim has ever surfaced. While true Ross made American flags in the late 1770s, the story of her being the creator of the very first flag is likely untrue and the creator of the first banner is lost to history.

FRANCES PERKINS

Perkins was the first female US Cabinet member. She served as Secretary of Labor under FDR. Perkins is also the second longest serving Cabinet member in history.

She played an essential role in the New Deal Program as well as she helped pull the labor movement into the New Deal coalition. Perkins championed many New Deal initiatives like the Civilian Conservation Corps, and The Public Works Administration. She helped establish unemployment benefits, elderly pension, Welfare, minimum wage, overtime laws and the establishment of the maximum 44 hour work week. She worked tirelessly to reduce workplace accidents and helped craft child labor laws as well as formed policy dealing with labor unions and alleviating strikes through the US Conciliation Service. The US Labor Department building is named after her in her honor.

MILDRED ELLA "BABE" DIDRIKSON ZAHARIAS

Babe Didrikson was an American athlete who achieved a great deal of success in golf, basketball and track and field. She won two gold medals in track and field at the 1932 Summer Olynpics before turning to professional golf and winning 10 LPGA major championships beginning in 1935.

Although a latecomer to the sport she quickly became the most famous being America's first female Golf celebrity and leading player of the 1940s and early 1950s. So proficient in the sport, Babe competed in the Los Angeles Open, a men's PGA tournament, a feat no other woman attempted until Annika Sorenstam, Suzy Whaley and Michelle Wie almost six decades later. Whatever women's sports was to become, much credit should be given to Babe Didrikson for allying any doubts that women could compete in athletics and women's sports was here to stay.

MYTH BUSTER ALERT!
GUSTAVE WHITEHEAD

Did history get who really invented the airplane "Wright"?

Born Gustav Albin Weisskopf, Gustave Whitehead was an aviation pioneer who emigrated from Germany to the US where he designed and built gliders, flying machines and engines between 1897 and 1915. A published newspaper article of the day suggested that he flew a powered machine successfully several times in 1901 and 1902, before the first flights by the Wright Brothers in 1903.

The account was written as an eyewitness report and described a powered and sustained flight by Whitehead in Connecticut on 14 August 1901. Dozens of newspapers in the U.S. and around the world soon repeated information from the article. Several local newspapers also reported on this and other flight experiments that Whitehead purportedly made in 1901 and in following years. Whitehead's aircraft designs and experiments were described or mentioned in contemporary *Scientific American* magazine articles and a 1904 book about industrial progress. His public profile faded after about 1915 and he died in relative obscurity in 1927. The feat is celebrated in Connecticut to this day as the real first successful air flight. So does history owe Gustave an apology? Seems so.

-Air & Space Magazine

PHILO FARNSWORTH

Many people credit Bill Gates and Steve Jobs for having the biggest impact on the information age, however the person that probably deserves more credit than any other for connecting America to the outside world is Philo Farnsworth.

Farnsworth is the brains behind the creation of the television.

At the age of 14, he figured out a way to transmit images electronically. In 1921, young Philo first described and diagrammed television in a school science paper.

In 1926, Farnsworth built his first television camera and receiving apparatus. A year later, he made the first electronic transmission of television, using a carbon arc projector to send a single line to a receiver in the next room of his apartment.

Unfortunately for Farnsworth, the Radio Corporation of America (RCA) owned a patent for television by a competing inventor. As a result, Farnsworth spent years of his life embroiled in lawsuits, defending himself from infringement claims and seeking to guard his own patent rights. In 1939, RCA finally licensed Farnsworth's patents and paid the inventor $1 million

Farnsworth only appeared on TV once on the game shown *I've Got A Secret*, in which a panel tries to guess his identity. Needless to say, they blow it.

WILLIE JAMES PERRY

While many people have made little recognized contributions to the fabric of American history, contributions that affected the nation as a whole, scores more have made contributions to their communities that also deserve recognition.

One such American was Willie Perry of Birmingham Alabama. I've included his story here to represent all those Americans that have made life better for us all while expecting nothing in return. I have also been a personal recipient of Willie's kindness.

Willie James Perry, also known as the Birmingham Batman was well-known for cruising around Birmingham helping stranded motorists and giving free rides in his customized 1971 Ford Thunderbird, dubbed the "Batmobile Rescue Ship".

Perry lived by the motto "Do unto others as you would have them do unto you." After he heard about a woman whose car had broken down being raped by a group of men who had seemingly stopped to help her, he decided to take to the streets in a way that he could be recognized as a helper that could be trusted.

Willie would travel around town carrying gas, jumper cables and tools to help people whose cars had broken down. He gave rides to people who had too much to drink, took elderly people to doctor's appointments and drove kids without transportation to fast food restaurants or as entertainment for birthday parties. He visited home-bound neighbors and assisted with guiding traffic around road hazards.

On at least one occasion Perry foiled an attempted robbery at a pharmacy. He always refused any offer of payment for his services.

Ironically it was Willie's caring generosity that contributed to his death. Willie Perry died in January 1985 of carbon monoxide poisoning while working on the Batmobile in an enclosed garage.

HERMAN HOLLERITH

Herman Hollerith was an American inventor of German descent who developed an electromechanical punched card tabulator to assist in summarizing information and, later, accounting. He was the founder of the Tabulating Machine Company that in 1911 was consolidated with three other companies to form the Computing-Tabulating-Recording Company, later renamed IBM.

Hollerith is regarded as one of the seminal figures in the development of data processing. His invention of the punched card tabulating machine marks the beginning of the era of semiautomatic data processing systems, and his concept dominated that landscape for nearly a century.

But this is not where the story ends, for it was Hollerith's punch card technology that was employed by the Nazi's during World War II to track and catalog Jews for asset removal and later extermination. Most assuredly without his knowledge nor consent.

(See *IBM and the Nazi Death Camps* in "Unknown" Military History)

3

Unknown Americana

Little known facts about life in America

HartofAmerica.net

DID YOU KNOW...

- 1 in 8 Americans have been employed by the fast food chain McDonald's
- In more than half of all U.S. states, the highest paid public employee in the state is a football coach.
- It costs the U.S. government 1.8 cents to mint a penny and 9.4 cents to mint a nickel.
- As an aspiring actor, Leonard Nimoy, yes Spock, worked as a cabbie. He once gave a ride to a future President of the United States... John Fitzgerald Kennedy.
- America is one of only two countries in the world, alongside New Zealand, that allows pharmaceutical companies to advertise prescription drugs directly to consumers. So all those Ambien and Zoloft commercials seem pretty odd to non-Americans.
- The phrase "Winning Hands Down" originally referred to a Jockey that won a race without whipping his horse or having to pull back on the reins.
- The equivalent of 100 Acres of Pizza are served in the US every day!
- By the time a child graduates from High School, he has seen 40,000 murders on TV. Concerns about the impact of television violence on society have been hotly debated for years. As early as 1952, the United States House of Representatives was holding hearings to explore the impact of television violence and concluded that the "television broadcast industry was a perpetrator and a deliverer of violence."

THE ORIGIN OF SIDEBURNS

The term SIDEBURNS is a 19th-century corruption of the original BURN-SIDES, named after American Civil War General Ambrose Burnsides. "Burnsides" became "sideburns" probably because of their location on the side of the face.

GENDER BIAS?

Often referred to as Ladies' Night This promotional event, often at a bar or nightclub, where women pay less than men for the cover charge or drinks has been subject of a debate in many state courts. In California, Maryland, Pennsylvania and Wisconsin courts have ruled that ladies' night discounts are unlawful gender discrimination under state or local statutes.

TWISTING THE NIGHT AWAY

When the popular game "Twister" was introduced in 1966, critics denounced the game as "sex in a box"

DAYLIGHT SAVINGS TIME

The original concept we now call Daylight Savings Time was an idea of Benjamin Franklin. Franklin published an essay in the Journal de Paris in April in 1784, called "An Economical Project for Diminishing the Cost of Light," where he proposed the French could conserve 64 million pounds of candle wax if they woke up with the sun in springtime' making the most of the natural daylight.

First introduced to the U.S. in 1918, "Fast Time" as it was called then, was signed into law by President Woodrow Wilson to support the war effort during the first World War. Seven months later the time change was repealed. However, some cities, including Pittsburgh, Boston, and New York, continued to use it until President Franklin D. Roosevelt instituted year-round DST in 1942.

SNAKE BIT SON?

Abraham Lincoln's son, Robert, is the only man in U.S. history to have witnessed the assassinations of three different Presidents, his father, James Garfield, and William McKinley. After he saw anarchist Leon Czolgosz shoot McKinley, he vowed he would never again appear in public with an incumbent President.

STATUE OF LIBERTY
The seven spikes on the crown of "Miss Liberty" represent the seven oceans and the seven continents of the world, indicating the universal concept of liberty. Although you cannot see Lady Liberty's feet clearly she is in fact standing among a broken shackle and chains, with her right foot raised, depicting her moving forward away from oppression and slavery.

WHAT'S IN A NAME?
In 1869, President Ulysses Grant Pardoned Dr. Samuel Mudd, the Doctor that set the broken ankle of Lincoln Assassin John Wilkes Booth while Booth was on the run. Some believe Mudd's reputation was so tarnished following the incident, it inspired the phrase "Your name is Mud". Although the origin of the phrase has been debated, there is no doubt it gained in popularity after the revelation Dr. Mudd assisted Booth. In fairness to the good Doctor It is not known if Mudd knew of Booths crime. But he was vilified as an accomplice just the same.

PRESIDENTIAL COINCIDENCE?
Much has been written about the coincidences between Abraham Lincoln and John Kennedy and their assassinations. But these coincidences are so compelling they deserve mentioning again.

1. Both men had seven letters in their last names
2. Both were shot in the head on Friday
3. Both were seated next to their wives when killed
4. Lincoln was shot at Ford's Theater. Kennedy was shot in a Lincoln limo which was made by Ford
5. Lincoln was in box 7 at Ford's theater and Kennedy was in car number 7 of the Dallas motorcade
6. Both assassins have three names with 15 letters John Wilkes Booth and Lee Harvey Oswald
7. Booth shot Lincoln in a theater and was captured in a warehouse Oswald shot Kennedy from a warehouse and was captured in a theater

8. Both were elected to the US House of Representatives for the first time in the year "46" 1846 and 1946 respectively and both were runners-up for their party's nomination for Vice President in the years of "56".
9. Both were succeeded by Southern Democrats name Johnson, each of whom had served as their respective VP's

DID YOU KNOW: MORE ODD FACTS

*   During Prohibition, the US Government, in an effort to persuade Americans to swear off booze, poisoned some alcohol with the intent of making people sick. The result? Over 10,000 people died.
*   Russia and the United States are only 55 miles apart at the Bering Strait off the West coast of Alaska.
*   Tweets, those ubiquitous 140 character "Micro Blogs" on the Social Media platform Twitter are all archived in the Library of Congress... Careful what you type, not only are you making history, you're leaving evidence.
*   In 1893 an Amendment was proposed to the US Constitution that would change the name of The United States of America, to The United States of the Earth. The proposed Amendment was from U.S. Representative Lucas Miller of Wisconsin, who said America should change its name based on his claim that;'It is possible for the Republic to grow through the admission of new States into the Union until every Nation on Earth has become part of it,' Miller, wasn't nominated for a second term. (Constitutionfacts.com)
*   The US tax code is roughly 5000 pages long. Whereas the longest book ever written War and Peace by Leo Tolstoy, and the Bible are roughly only 4500
*   During the second World War the Federal Government banned sliced bread as a war time conservation effort. The ban was ordered by Claude Wickard who held the position of Food Administrator. According to the NEW YORK TIMES, officials explained that

"the ready-sliced loaf must have a heavier wrapping than an un-sliced one if it is not to dry out." It was also intended to counteract a rise in the price of bread, caused by the Office of Price Administrations authorization of a ten percent increase in flour prices.

NO TEXTING WAS INVOLVED

The First automobile Accident involving a gasoline-powered car occurred in Ohio City, Ohio in 1891. The driver, engineer James Lambert was driving one of his inventions, a gasoline-powered buggy, when he ran into a little trouble. The buggy, also carrying a passenger hit a tree root sticking out of the ground. Lambert lost control and the vehicle swerved and crashed into a hitching post. Both men suffered minor injuries.

THAT'S ONE BIG BRIDGE

The Golden Gate bridge, in San Francisco uses longest bridge cables ever made. Long enough to circle the world at the equator 3 times. They are so big and heavy they had to be fabricated on site.

THE ELECTRICITY WARS

Went into full swing in the early 20th Century with animal electrocutions common. Topsy the elephant was electrocuted at Luna Park Zoo on Coney Island in 1903. Captured on film by Thomas Edison, the event was one of a string of such demonstrations Edison staged to discredit a new form of emerging electricity: alternating current, which, if it posed any immediate danger at all, was to only the future of Edison's own direct current.

Edison had established direct current at the standard for electricity distribution and was living very comfortably off the patent royalties, royalties he was concerned about losing when George Westinghouse and Nicola Tesla introduced alternating current. Hence the sacrifice of animals in an attempt to discredit the competition. The public displays came to be known as the Electricity Wars.

20 SECONDS TO DISASTER

The successful Apollo 11 moon landing on July 20, 1969, ushered in an era of moon exploration that has so far gone unrivaled. However "11" was less than a minute short of disaster as it only had 20 seconds worth of fuel left to "stick" the moon landing. As the craft started its approach, Buzz Aldrin and Neil Armstrong got into the lunar module and began their descent. The close call was likely due to a change of plans by Armstrong. According to Aldrin…

"Neil didn't like what we were heading toward, and we selected a safer spot alongside a crater with boulders in it. We landed with a little less fuel than we would have liked to have had, maybe 20 seconds of fuel left."

THE BATTLE OF ATHENS TENNESSEE

Shortly after WWII Voter fraud was running rampant throughout much of the Deep South, with forged ballots and secret vote counts commonplace. In 1946 in McMinn County Tennessee the frustration reached its boiling point. Although Federal authorities were asked to intervene, the calls for oversight fell on deaf ears. And in early August of 1946, the locals used armed force to ensure a fair outcome in local elections.

Here's how it went down…

In 1936 a man named Paul Cantrell was elected sheriff for the first of 3 times. He was elected state senator in '42 and '44. One of Cantrell's associates, a man named Pat Mansfield, was elected sheriff while Cantrell served in the Tennessee State Senate. But in 1946, Cantrell decided he wanted the office of sheriff back.

But Cantrell was about to meet with some unanticipated opposition.

After the end of WWII, some 3,000 veterans, returned home to McMinn County. These veterans, seasoned by hard fighting in the European and Pacific theaters of war, decided to put up one of their own to run as a candidate for sheriff in the primary election against Cantrell. These ex-GIs promised honest elections to the voters as a part of their reform plan for the county government.

During the primary election, 200 armed men were brought in by the local political machine to act as "deputies" at the polls.

Newly returned veteran Poll-watchers were not allowed into the area where ballots were to be counted, and Sheriff Mansfield ordered his "deputies" to disperse the public. One of the deputies raised his gun and called out, "If you sons of bitches cross this street I'll kill you!"

Not to be intimidated, The GIs decided to find themselves some weapons and take matters into their own hands. The National Guard and State Guard armories had American M-1 rifles, British Enfield rifles, and some .45 caliber pistols.

On August 2nd, the GIs bombed the jail with dynamite, and the deputies surrendered. They then took control of the jail and held the deputies overnight, until calm was restored to the town. With the ballots counted fairly the GI candidate for sheriff, Knox Henry, won election by a 3-to-2 margin.

The skirmish became known as the Battle of Athens and demonstrated how American patriots can restore the rule of law, by legitimately ousting corrupt, politicians, by force of arms. The Battle of Athens stands as an example of what patriotic Americans can do to protect themselves from government tyranny.

A GOOD CORPORATE CITIZEN
During the Dust Bowl, people sewed clothes out of flour sacks when money was tight. When flour distributors heard about this, they began making their bags more colorful so the subsequent clothing would be more attractive.

DRIVING ON A RUNWAY
The US Interstate Highway System requires that every fifth mile has to be straight so that these sections can be used as airstrips in times of war.

GOT A TISSUE?
Kleenex tissues were actually developed for use as gasmask filters during World War 1

A CONCEPT UP IN SMOKE, LITERALLY!

New York's Empire State Building was designed for docking passenger laden airships. The architects who designed the building envisioned that airships would anchor to the buildings spire and passengers could descend via gangplank to the 102nd floor. Then on May 6, 1937 the Hindenburg exploded, and the airship concept was abandoned. Their descendants, lighter weight blimps, were relegated to high flying billboards and providing aerial coverage of sporting events.

HOORAY FOR HOLLYWOOD

When the now iconic Hollywood Sign was first erected, in 1923 it was meant to be temporary and the original version actually read "Hollywoodland." The sign was meant to be part of an 18-month advertising campaign to attract home buyers to the Los Angeles area.

In the late 1940s, "land" was removed and for decades, the Sign slipped into a state of disrepair. In August of 1978, the landmark was demolished, leaving the peak bare for three months, until a new Hollywood sign was unveiled 3 months later. The Hollywood sign has a dark side as well.

In 1932 24-year-old Peg Entwistle jumped to her death off of the 'H' believing her dreams of become a movie star would never materialize. According to the LA Times, a hiker found her body, along with a handwritten suicide note, in a ravine below. Ironically, a letter arrived for Entwistle a few days later. She was accepted into the Bliss-Hayden School of Acting specifically for a role as a young woman who, ironically enough, commits suicide.

THINGS YOU DID NOT KNOW ABOUT THE STAR SPANGLED BANNER

Francis Scott Key actually intended his verses to be song lyrics, not poetry. Contrary to popular belief, "The Star Spangled-Banner" was not a poem set to a melody years later. Although Key was an amateur poet, when he composed his verses, he intended them to accompany a popular song of the day. Key wanted the words to be sung to the melody of "To Anacreon in Heaven." Although Key composed the patriotic lyrics amid much anti-British euphoria, "To Anacreon in Heaven" was ironically an English song that served as the theme song of the upper-crust Anacreontic Society of London (A gentlemen's club of musicians, Doctors, and other "intellectual" professions) and a popular pub staple.

MYTH BUSTER ALERT!

Contrary to popular lore Key was not imprisoned on a British warship when he wrote the verses.

Key, a Washington, D.C., lawyer, had been sent by President James Madison on a mission to Baltimore to negotiate for the release of Dr. William Beanes, a prominent surgeon captured at the Battle of Bladensburg. Along with John Stuart Skinner, a fellow lawyer working for the State Department, Key set sail on an American sloop and on September 7 the two boarded the British ship Tonnant, where they secured the prisoner's release under one condition—they could not go ashore until after the British attacked Baltimore. Accompanied by British guards on September 10, Key returned to the American sloop from which he witnessed the bombardment of Fort McHenry

The song was not originally entitled "The Star-Spangled Banner."

When Key scrawled his lyrics on the back of a letter he did not give them any title. Within a week, Key's verses were printed on broadsides and in Baltimore newspapers with the title "Defense of Fort McHenry." In November, a Baltimore music store printed the patriotic song with sheet music for the first time under the more lyrical title "The Star-Spangled Banner."

The flag Key "hailed at the twilight's last gleaming" did not fly "through the perilous fight."

The night of the bombardment a torrent of rain fell on Fort McHenry during the Battle of Baltimore. The fort's 30-by-42-foot garrison flag was so massive that it required 11 men to hoist when dry, and if waterlogged the woolen banner could have weighed upwards of 500 pounds and snapped the flagpole. So as the rain poured down, a smaller storm flag that measured 17-by-25 feet flew in its place. "In the morning they most likely took down the rain-soaked storm flag and hoisted the bigger one and that's the flag Key saw in the morning.

It did not become the national anthem until more than a century after it was written.

Along with "Hail Columbia" and "Yankee Doodle," "The Star-Spangled Banner" was among the prevalent patriotic airs in the aftermath of the War of 1812. During the Civil War, "The Star-Spangled Banner" was an anthem for Union troops, and the song increased in popularity in the ensuing decades, which led to President Woodrow Wilson signing an executive order in 1916 designating it as "the national anthem of the United States" for all military ceremonies. On March 3, 1931, after 40 previous attempts failed, a measure passed Congress and was signed into law that formally designated "The Star-Spangled Banner" as the national anthem of the United States.

-The History Channel

Only 25% is "Anthem"

Most people do not realize that our National Anthem is just the first verse of Key's song. When we sing this ballad at ball games, parades and other civic events, we're leaving 3 of the songs remaining verses.

Here's the Star Spangled Banner in it's entirety:

Oh, say can you see, by the dawn's early light, What so proudly we hailed at the twilight's last gleaming? Whose broad stripes and bright stars, through the perilous fight, O'er the ramparts we watched, were so gallantly streaming? And the rockets' red glare, the bombs bursting in air, Gave proof through the night that our flag was still there. O say, does that star-spangled banner yet wave O'er the land of the free and the home of the brave?

On the shore, dimly seen through the mists of the deep, Where the foe's haughty host in dread silence reposes, What is that which the breeze, o'er the towering steep, As it fitfully blows, half conceals, half discloses? Now it catches the gleam of the morning's first beam, In full glory reflected now shines on the stream: 'Tis the star-spangled banner! O long may it wave O'er the land of the free and the home of the brave.

And where is that band who so vauntingly swore, that the havoc of war and the battle's confusion A home and a country should leave us no more? Their blood has wiped out their foul footstep's pollution. No refuge could save the hireling and slave, from the terror of flight, or the gloom of the grave: And the star-spangled banner in triumph doth wave. O'er the land of the free and the home of the brave.

Oh! thus be it ever, when freemen shall stand between their loved homes and the war's desolation! Blest with victory and peace, may the heaven-rescued land Praise the Power that hath made and preserved us a nation. Then conquer we must, when our cause it is just, and this be our motto: "In God is our trust."And the star-spangled banner in triumph shall wave, O'er the land of the free and the home of the brave!

WHAT'S IN A NAME? SCOOBY

Frank Sinatra is arguably the most famous member of the Rat Pack. But did you know that Sinatra's hit, "Strangers In The Night," actually inspired the name for one of our most beloved cartoon characters? Iwao Takamoto, who animated Scooby-Doo, got the inspiration for Scooby's name after listening to Sinatra's ad-libbed "Dooby dooby doo," scat at the end of the song!

4

Unknown Military History

Odd plans, little known events, and bizarre ideas in defense of America

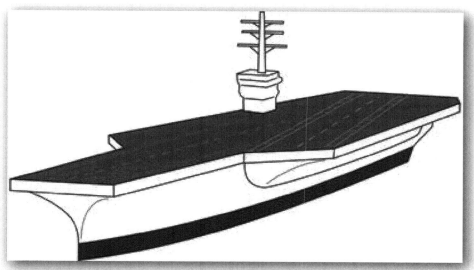

HartofAmerica.net

...AND NO REWARD WAS EVEN OFFERED

When George Washington found a lost dog during the battle of Germantown, he crossed enemy lines to return the wayward K9 to its rightful owner, General Howe, his opponent in the battle.

PROSTITUTING THE WAR

During the Civil War Union General Joseph Hooker brought prostitutes along for his soldiers to keep them sexually satisfied. His legacy is so (in)famous that his name is now synonymous with the world's oldest profession.

THE OTHER JEFFERSON DAVIS

The Union had their own Jefferson Davis. Union General Davis shared a name with the Confederate President, a circumstance that didn't cause as much confusion with one notable exception. It was during the Battle of Chickamauga in 1863, as darkness fell on Horseshoe Ridge, members of the 21st Ohio saw a swarm of men approaching but couldn't tell if they were friend or foe. Most assumed they were Union reinforcements, but a few feared they were Confederates. As the troops grew closer, one Union soldier called out, "What troops are you?" The collective reply was "Jeff Davis's troops." The Ohio soldiers relaxed, believing they meant the Union general. A few moments later, they were staring down the muzzles and bayonets of the 7th Florida. The Ohioans surrendered. The Confederates won that battle.

   -smithsonianmag.org

THE THEATRICS OF WAR

Deception in combat is not unusual and this certainly applies to the US Civil War. At Corinth Mississippi in May of 1862 Confederate General P.T.G. Beauregard pulled a fast one on the Union Troops. Outnumbered two to one and expecting a massive Union assault at daybreak, Beauregard ordered a single locomotive rolled in and out of the town all night making it sound as if thousands of fresh troops were arriving on an endless procession of trains. To add to the charade, he had his men cheer each time the lone steam engine pulled into the station, fooling the Yankees into believing the reinforced Southerners were amassing in droves. Meanwhile, Beauregard was evacuating the town; the sound of the train even masking the noise of his army breaking camp.

THE CIVIL "WARS"

The US Civil War was known by more than 25 names, including "The Brothers War," "The War to Suppress Yankee Arrogance," "The War for the Union," "The War of the Rebellion, War for Southern Independence, The War between the States, The War of Northern Aggression, The War of Southern Aggression, The Freedom War, The War of Secession, The Battle between North and South side of the United States, American (US) North-South War", The War for Emancipation, and numerous others and often depending on the of the perspective of the person or people discussing it.

ENLISTED ELEPHANTS

In one of the stranger events of the Civil War, President Abraham Lincoln politely declined an offer of war elephants from the King of Siam. While the letter from Rama IV was actually addressed to the previous President James Buchanan, it was up to Lincoln and his Secretary of State William Seward to politely decline this rather bizarre offer. As Lincoln pointed out in his reply to Rama, steam power had overtaken the need for heavy animal power of this kind.

LINCOLN'S ODD CURRENCY

After President Abraham Lincoln died, on April 15, 1865, his leather wallet was found to contain a $5 Confederate bill, imprinted with the image of Confederate President Jefferson Davis. Lincoln may have gotten the bill when he visited Richmond earlier that month.

THE LUSITANIA SINKING, INTENTIONAL?

In early May 1915, several New York newspapers published a warning by the Germans that Americans traveling on British or Allied ships in war zones did so at their own risk. The announcement was placed on the same page as an advertisement of the imminent sailing of the Lusitania liner from New York back to Liverpool. The sinkings of merchant ships off the south coast of Ireland prompted the British Admiralty to warn the Lusitania to avoid the area.

Some historians contend the vessels provocative route was set intentionally to provoke the attack which occurred on May 7th 1915 and create further justification for the US involvement in the war. Especially after it was revealed that the Lusitania was carrying about 173 tons of war munitions for Britain, which the Germans cited as justification for the attack.

Of the more than 1,900 passengers and crew members on board, more than 1,100 perished, including 128 Americans. Nearly two years would pass before the United States formally entered World War I, but the sinking of the Lusitania played a significant role in turning public opinion against Germany, both in the United States and abroad.

MR. AND MRS. TANK

At the beginning of the World War 1, tanks were grouped according to their 'gender'. The male tanks had cannons attached while the females carried machine guns. The prototype tank was named Little Willie.

HITLER INVADES AMERICA

During the Second World War, Adolph Hitler launched a failed mission to strike fear into the heart of America when the German Dictator attempted to terrorize the US by infiltrating America with spies. The first setback-back came when a Nazi U-boat carrying secret agents got wedged 400 yards off the coast of New York.

The submarine ran aground on a sandbar off Long Island as its commander attempted to drop off four agents. The mission was codenamed Operation Pastorious. The intention of the mission was to bomb a string of targets and see the U.S. 'burning in flames'. Targets included New York's Pennsylvania station, the city's water supply power plants, bridges and Jewish-owned department stores.

The mission was a dismal failure but was not the only attempt by the Nazi's to invade US shores. Over the years reports of German U Boats in places like the Hudson River, the Gulf of Mexico and others were plentiful although many of these sightings we're unconfirmed. However it is known that the Nazi's did in fact attempt to bring the war to America, although with little success.

ANTI-SEMITISM OR JUST POOR JUDGMENT?

Before the Nazi Holocaust ramped up to full speed, Adolph Hitler gave the US, Britain and several other European nations the opportunity to take Jewish refugees; while many were accepted, many more were not.

After Germany annexed Austria in March 1938, nations in western Europe and the Americas feared an influx of Jewish refugees. About 85,000 Jewish refugees reached the United States between March 1938 and September 1939, but this number was far below the number seeking refuge. In 1938, 125,000 applicants applied for the 27,000 visas under the existing immigration quota. And the refugees kept coming to escape Hitler.

In a highly publicized event in the Spring of 1939, the United States refused to admit over 900 Jewish refugees who had sailed from Hamburg, Germany, on the St. Louis.

After Cuban authorities canceled the refugees' transit visas and denied entry to most of the passengers, The St. Louis sailed for America. Many on board were still waiting to receive visas to enter the United States.

But the US denied permission for the St. Louis to make port and the ship was forced to return to Europe. The governments of Great Britain, France, the Netherlands, and Belgium, already taxed with their own influx of refugees, agreed to accept some of the passengers. But of the 908 St. Louis passengers who denied entry into the US, 254 are known to have died in the Holocaust.

During the second half of 1941, even as unconfirmed reports of the mass murder perpetrated by the Nazis made their way to the West, the US Department of State placed even stricter limits on immigration based on national security concerns. So the total number of Jews that perished due to these restrictions is likely considerably higher.

(The United States Holocaust Memorial Museum)

IBM AND NAZI DEATH CAMPS

When Adolph Hitler came to power, a central Nazi goal was to identify and destroy Germany's roughly half million Jews. To Nazis, Jews were not just those who practiced Judaism, but those of Jewish blood, intermarriage, religious activity, or even conversion to Christianity. Only after Jews were identified could they be targeted for asset confiscation, ghettoization, deportation, and ultimately extermination. To search generations of communal, church, and governmental records all across Germany-and later throughout Europe-was a cross-indexing task so monumental, it called for a computer. But in 1933, no computer existed.

However, another invention did exist: the IBM punch card and card sorting system-a precursor to the computer. This technology was invented by Herman Hollerith who was an American inventor of German descent. Hollerith developed an electromechanical punched card tabulator to assist in summarizing information and, later, accounting. He was the founder of the Tabulating Machine Co. that was consolidated in 1911 with three other companies to form the Computing Tabulating Recording Co., later renamed IBM.

IBM, primarily through its German subsidiary, made Hitler's program of Jewish destruction possible. IBM Germany, designed, executed, and supplied the technological assistance Hitler's Third Reich needed. More than 2,000 such multi-machine sets were dispatched throughout Germany, and thousands more throughout German-dominated Europe. Card sorting operations were established in every major concentration camp. People were moved from place to place, and their remains catalogued with icy automation.

Although historians, Holocaust experts and WWII buffs have debated for decades the extent of IBM's knowledge and complicity. It is commonly accepted that had it not been for IBM's punch card technology, Hitler's

"Final Solution" would not have been nearly as horrifically successful as it was. (jewishvirtuallibrary.org)

THE "BOO" BATTALION
The Ghost Army was a US Army tactical deception unit during the Second World War. Officially known as the 23rd Headquarters Special Troops, the 1,100-man unit was given a unique mission: to impersonate other U.S. Army units to deceive the enemy. From a few weeks after D-Day when they landed in France until the end of the war, they put on a "traveling road show" utilizing inflatable thanks, sound trucks, and fake radio transmissions. The unit staged more than 20 battlefield deceptions, often operating very close to the front lines. Their story was kept secret for more than 40 years after the war, and elements of it remain classified to this day.

DON'T FORGET TO CHANGE YOUR PASSWORD...
Is a constant reminder in this day of cyber security. The bane of many, keeping up with passwords to protect of most personal data is an ongoing task, however the US Government has not always shared that concern. For over 20 years the launch code for all Minute Man Nuclear missiles was the same; 00000000. Steven Bellovin a computer science professor at Columbia, uncovered the startling fact after finding a 2004 paper by Dr. Bruce G. Blair, a former Air Force officer who manned Minuteman silos.

The codes — known as Permissive Action Links (PALs) — were meant to give only the president of the United States the power to use such weapons. Apparently, this security feature was largely symbolic. For two decades, multiple presidents carried around a briefcase that supposedly contained constantly changing launch codes, though it may as well have been filled with shredded newspaper as each knew the not so complex and never changing code, by heart.

A GAY BOMB?
The "halitosis bomb" and "gay bomb" are informal names for two theoretical non-lethal chemical weapons that the United States Air Force research

laboratory speculated about producing; the theories involve discharging female sex pheromones over enemy forces in order to make them sexually attracted to each other and therefore unlikely to fight since they would be too "Busy".

THAT'S A LOT OF WARDROBE CHANGES
Among the first "Germans" captured at Normandy were several Koreans. They had been forced to fight for the Japanese Army until they were captured by the Russians and forced to fight for the Russian Army until they were captured by the Germans and forced to fight for the German Army until they were captured by the US Army.

THEY STOLE OUR INSIGNIA
For the first 15 years of its existence, members of the 45th Infantry Division wore a swastika on their left shoulders. The symbol was actually an ancient American Indian symbol of good luck. The insignia served as recognition of the large number of Native Americans serving in the 45th Infantry Division. The yellow swastika was on a square background of red symbolizing the Spanish Heritage of the 4 Southwestern states that made up the membership of the 45th—Oklahoma, New Mexico, Colorado, and Arizona. A similar symbol was adopted by the Nazi party in the late 1920's, and as the Nazi's rose to power in 1933 the symbol became so closely associated with German socialism that it was abandoned as the insignia of the 45th Infantry Division.

K-9 CORPS
Well over a million dogs served on both sides during World War I, carrying messages along the network of trenches and providing some measure of psychological comfort to the soldiers. The most famous was Rin Tin Tin, an abandoned puppy of German war dogs found in France in 1918 and taken to the United States, where he made his film debut in the 1922 silent film The Man from Hell's River.

In the United States, the practice of training dogs for military purposes was abandoned after World War I. But when the country entered World War II in December 1941, the American Kennel Association and a group called Dogs for Defense began a movement to mobilize dog owners to donate healthy and capable animals to the Quartermaster Corps of the U.S. Army. Training began in March 1942, and that fall the QMC was given the task of training dogs for the U.S. Navy, Marines and Coast Guard as well.

There are about 2500 dogs in active service today and about 700 deployed overseas.

THE NEVER ENDING WAR

The Korean war is still "Officially" being fought. The Korean Armistice Agreement between the US, North Korea, The Korean People's Army and the Chinese Peoples Volunteer Army was signed on July 27, 1953, and was designed to insure a complete cessation of hostilities and of all acts of armed force in Korea until a final peaceful settlement was achieved. No "final peaceful settlement" has been achieved to date and so in the legal sense the Korean war continues to this day.

COLD WAR KITTY

Operation Acoustic Kitty was a project launched by the CIA's Agency Directorate of Science and Technology, which in the 1960s intended to use felines to spy on the Kremlin and Soviet embassies. So here was the plan; a veterinary surgeon implanted a microphone into a cat's ear canal, a small radio transmitter at the base of its skull and a thin wire into its fur. This would allow the cat to secretly record and transmit audio from its surroundings. Due to problems with distraction, the cat's sense of hunger had to be addressed in another operation. The project was finally cancelled in 1967 after being deemed a failure and complete loss. Former CIA officer, named Victor Marchetti estimated that Project Acoustic Kitty cost about 20 million dollars.

ON DASHER, ON DANCER, ON PRANCER ON VIXEN

On December 24, 1955, a newspaper advertisement told children that they could call Santa and listed a number. The number was incorrect and the calls went to private line at the US Air Defense Command. The senior officer on duty was Colonel Harry Shoup. Shoup instructed his team to give the kids Santa's "current location." Due to that one incident, a tradition began, and now a program called "NORAD Tracks Santa" enlists volunteers to track Santa's flight across the world on Christmas Eve to the delight of kids of all ages.

VAMPIRE DRONES

During the second world war "Bat Bombs" were proposed to the US military by a dental surgeon. Because bats can carry a large amount of weight the plan was to make an army of flying suicide bombers and release them over Japan. The rodent Kamikazes had napalm explosive kits made for them, and then special cases were constructed that would be dropped from B-29s, releasing the bats.

The plan began to draw criticism when some armed bats were accidentally released and set up shop under a fuel tank on an Air Force base, which exploded and burned to the ground.

But given the accident, optimism remained considering the bomb casings they'd made for the bats could hold over 1,000 bats, it was estimated just one bomber could hold up to 200,000 little flaming night terrors and some initial test data concluded these bat bombs were actually superior to regular fire bombs.

But after over two million dollars in funding, the plan was scrapped. It was moving forward too slowly, and the bats deemed to be just too unpredictable.

5

Unknown Sports

Weird Stats and facts from the playing field

HartofAmerica.net

QUICK SPRINTS

- Jordan Spieth won just $61,867 less at one Masters PGA Tournament than Arnold Palmer won in his entire career.
- Roger Bannister held the world record in the mile for exactly 46 days
- There are only about 18 minutes of actual play in a regular 9 inning Baseball game.
- Princess Anne, Daughter of Queen Elizabeth II, did not have to undergo gender verification at the 1976 Olympics due to "Royal Courtesy"
- When asked why he didn't win Gold in Cross Country at the 2010 Olympics, Norwegian Skier Odd-Bjoern Hjelmeset said, "I think I have seen too much porn in the last 14 days".
- The phrase about winning something "Hands down" originally referred to a jockey that won a race without whipping his horse or pulling back on the reins
- Only three men have won the NCAA title as both a player and a coach: Joe B Hall, Bobby Knight and Dean Smith.
- Horse racings Triple Crown has been achieved just three time since 1949, all within a six year span in the mid 1970's. Secretariat in 1973, Seattle Slew in 1977 and Affirmed in 1978
- Only 11 Hockey Goalies have scored a goal in the history of the NHL, with the first happening in 1979 and the last in 2013
- The PGA record for the highest score on a par 4 hole is 16, set by Kevin Nain in 2011
- Only 72 players in NBA History have attempted more Free Throws in their entire careers then the 5,317 that Shaquille O'Neal missed.
- The night before the "Miracle on Ice", American Goalie Jim Craig played the video game Centipede with Soviet Hockey Star Sergei Makarov at the Olympic Village
- Four US Presidents have been featured on the cover of Sports Illustrated: John F. Kennedy, Gerald Ford, Ronald Reagan (Twice) and Bill Clinton

- Only one city has won three major sports championships in the same year: Detroit in 1935, when the Lions won the NFL Title, The Tigers won the World Series and the Red Wings took the Stanley Cup.
- Wilt Chamberlain won three straight Big Eight Titles in the High Jump and was also inducted into the Volleyball Hall of Fame.
- While a player at Florida State, Lee Corso had a roommate named Burt Reynolds. Reynolds eventually dropped out of State because he was going "to Hollywood to be a movie star"
- Michael Jordan's nickname in high school was "Magic", after Magic Johnson
- The Longest recorded point in Tennis history was in a 1984 women's match. It took 29 minutes with the ball crossing the net 648 times.
- Only 10 Quarterbacks in NFL history have thrown half as many passes as Peyton Manning
- Roger Maris was never intentionally walked the year he hit 61 home runs. Presumably because Mickey Mantle batted next
- The Boston Bruins name is spelled "BQSTON BRUINS" on the Stanley Cup for their 1971-72 Title.
- Janet Hill the mother of NBA Player Grant Hill, who played for four teams in his pro career including the Detroit Pistons, Orlando Magic, Phoenix Suns, and Los Angeles Clippers, roomed with Hillary Clinton while attending Wellesley College.
- In 1991 Michael Jordan, Bo Jackson and Wayne Gretzky starred in a short lived Saturday morning cartoon called "Pro Stars"
- Major League Baseball umpires are required to wear black underwear while on the job in case they split their pants.

ROSIE "DOESN'T GO THE DISTANCE

In the 1980 Boston Marathon a 23-year-old Rosie Ruiz crossed the finish line with the third-fastest time ever for a female runner. The fact that Rosie appeared to have hardly broken a sweat in the grueling 26 mile event caused some spectators to wonder. That wariness was justified when a few onlookers reported that they saw Ruiz join the race in the final mile, where she sprinted to the finish line. She was stripped of her olive wreath and the rightful winner, Jacqueline Gareau, was crowned the Woman's winner.

IT'S YOGI BERRA ALL OVER AGAIN

In June of 1953 the Boston Red Sox destroyed the Detroit Tigers by a score of 17 to 1. The very next day the Tigers lost the rematch when, again the Sox managed to rack up 17 runs. What makes this story even more interesting is all the runs were scored in one inning in both games.

GOOD LUCK, JACK

Jack Nicklaus won his second Masters in 1965. In the very same year, the Montreal Canadiens took home the Stanley Cup, the NBA Championship was won by the Celtics, and Willie Shoemaker won the Kentucky Derby. In 1986, Nicklaus won his last Masters. Coincidently all three of these same events, happened again.

THE COMEBACK KID, AGAIN!

In 1984, quarterback Frank Reich recorded the most impressive comeback in the history of college football, when he led his team, the University of Maryland, to defeat the Miami Hurricanes after they were 31 points down.

Nine years later, the Buffalo Bills, who were 32 points down in their game against the Oilers, subbed an injured player for Reich, who came on the field to lead his team to the greatest comeback in professional football.

PASSING IS FOR PANSIES

In the 20th century before professional football existed and college football was all there was, an incomplete forward pass used to earn a team a 15-yard penalty. Not only that, but if the pass was incomplete and never touched, the defense then took possession of the ball. Though many coaches at the time regarded the forward pass as a rather "unmanly" way to play, the lower levels of contact that occurs during passing plays may have saved lives. In 1905, there were 18 football fatalities between high school and college leagues.

-"EXTINCT" OLYMPICS"-

Over the years many different sports have made their way into the Olympic line up. And over the years some competitions have been eliminated, and usually for good reason. Here are some of the stranger events that Olympic fans are no longer tortured by.

LIVE PIGEON SHOOTING

The live pigeon shooting event made its only Olympic appearance at the Paris Games in 1900.

SWIMMING OBSTACLE COURSE

Paris River Seine was the scene of the one and only 200-meter obstacle swimming race at the 1900 Games. Swimmers had to climb over a pole and row of boats before swimming under another row of vessels. Australia's Fred Lane took home the gold medal in the event, as well as finishing first in the 200 meter freestyle.

TUG OF WAR

Featured in five Olympic Games from Paris 1900 through to Antwerp 1920 (1916's Olympiad was cancelled after the outbreak of the first World War). Teams of eight men had five minutes to pull their opponents six feet over a line. If there was no winner after the time limit expired, the team who'd pulled their rivals the furthest would win.

LONG JUMP FOR HORSES

The first and only time was also in Paris in 1900. — The winner was Constant Van Langendonck of Belgium atop his mount Extra Dry. He won gold with a 6.10-meter leap.

CROQUET

As is the case with "extinct" Olympic Events The croquet appeared at the Olympics on just one occasion, It's notable for being the first Olympic event in which women were allowed to compete — although it was against their male counterparts and not in their own competition.

ROPE CLIMBING
Making an appearance at five Olympics from 1896 to 1932, competitors began from a seated position, using only their hands to climb up 49 feet at the Athens Games in 1896, but then the climb was changed to 25 feet in the later events.

-WHAT'S IN A NAME?-
Apparently for these sports teams, not much. Here are some of the, arguably, worse teams names from the Amateur ranks.

THE CHINKS
The town of Pekin, IL got its name because it's believed that it's located on the exact opposite side of the globe from Pekin, China, So, in light of this discovery they decide to name their athletic teams the Chinks. As sort of a backhanded salute to China. After finally coming to their senses they opted to renamed their teams, the Dragons.

HOT DOGS
Frankfort High School in Frankfort Indiana is home of this team. Despite the intimidating Weiner Dog Mascot, "The Dogs" stay in the perpetual losing season category.

HARDROCKERS
Although you probably thought it something different the Hardrockers suit up to represent The South Dakota School of Mines.

THE FIGHTING PLANETS
The brain trust at Mars High School in Pennsylvania, thought this a clever way to give a nod to the town. But just putting the word "Fighting" in front of any other word is not the way you name a team, unless, maybe you're from Mars!

THE CHOKERS
Grays Harbor College is a community college located in Aberdeen, Washington. This school fields men's teams for baseball and wrestling, women's teams for

soccer, softball and volleyball and men's and women's teams for basketball and golf. The name has not proven to be an omen as this Northwest Athletic Conference school earns their share of victories despite the name.

THE DIRTBAGS
This moniker is used exclusively for the Long Beach State baseball team. The nickname refers to the programs style of play and success against higher level teams. The name was first used in 1989 when LBS fielded it's first team and without a home field the team was forced to practice at an all dirt pony field. The schools official name is the 49'ers which all the other teams go by.

BANANA SLUGS
When Santa Cruz joined NCAA's Division III in 1981, athletic officials presented the school with its first official mascot: the sea lion. But the students were having none of it. After five years of dealing with the two-mascot problem, an overwhelming pro slug straw vote by students in 1986 persuaded the chancellor to make the Banana Slug UCSC's official mascot.

THE CRIMINALS
This nickname was originally an insult hurled at Yuma Union High by Phoenix Union High, after Yuma defeated Phoenix for the state football championship. Yuma adopted it as their official team name in 1917. Ironically, after a fire damaged the school in 1910 Yuma moved to the Yuma Territorial Prison for a brief "Incarceration"

THE CORNJERKERS
Referring to the motion that was used to harvest corn before the invention of modern machinery, this Hoopeston Illinois Area High School, has been resistant to keeping up with the times by perhaps considering a name change to say, the Combines.

THE VIOLETS
For more than a century, NYU athletes have worn violet and white in competition, which is the root of the nickname Violets. In the 1980s, after

briefly using a student dressed as a Violet for a mascot, the school adopted the bobcat as its mascot. A little more intimidating for a collegiate football team.

SPACE PIONEERS
The mascot of Indianapolis NW High School. The school, built in 1962, adopted the "Space Pioneer's as a nod to the United States early man in space program which was underway during the school's founding. And no the Junior Varsity team is not the Space Cadets.

THE MACON WHOOPEE
Located in Macon Georgia, the now defunct Whoopie was a professional hockey team that played from the mid 90's until 2001 in the Central Hockey League. Reportedly the Whoopee had no shortage of walk-ons looking for a chance to "make" the team.

6

Before America

What America looked like before it was America

HartofAmerica.net

MYTH BUSTER ALERT!
OUR "REAL" INDEPENDENCE DAY

Americans mistakenly celebrate our Independence on July 4th. However the day Congress voted for American Independence from British rule is actually July 2, 1776, not the 4th. July 4th is just when John Hancock put the first signature on the Declaration of Independence. (Which was actually a blank piece of paper when he signed it. His signature was added went the document went to print)

OUR FAMILY TREE

An estimated one tenth of American's could be a blood relative of one of the original 102 pilgrims who arrived at Plymouth Rock Massachusetts aboard the Mayflower in 1620.

ENGLAND PASSES

Sir Francis Drake, the English sea captain and explorer during the reign of Queen Elizabeth I, claimed the land on the west coast of North America for the Crown in 1579. His claim was valid by sixteenth century standards. He had obtained consent from local natives, and is thought to be the first European to discover the place, but as it turned out, the Crown wasn't much interested in the Pacific side of the New World. By the time the twentieth century rolled around, the event had been mainly forgotten, until 1936, when the discovery of an artifact in San Francisco Bay proved Drake's visit and the British claim on California, or New Albion as it was called at the time. Had the claim been accepted America could today have two "New Englands".

AN ARMY BEFORE AMERICA

The Battles of Lexington and Concord were fought by militias. (The men were famously called to arms by Paul Revere, who did not shout "The British are coming!" because most residents of Massachusetts considered themselves British.) Once it became clear that war was at hand, the Second Continental Congress authorized a Continental Army with a unified command structure, to be led by Major General George Washington. The measure passed on June 14, 1775, and is still celebrated as the Army's birthday. Meaning the United States Army pre-dates the United States. (The Continental Marines also predate the country having been founded on November 11 of the same year)

PARTY LIKE IT'S 1776

Two days before signing the Declaration of Independence, the delegates of the Constitutional Convention threw a party where they consumed 54 bottles of Madeira, 60 bottles of Claret, 8 bottles of fine Whiskey, 22 bottles of Porter, 8 bottles of hard cider, 12 beers, and 7 bowls of the Colonial version of "Hunch Punch"

THE WINDS OF WAR

The Revolutionary War nearly started earlier than it did thanks to Sarah Tarrant. Tarrant was a nurse with a fiery temper who lived in Salem, Massachusetts in 1775. When British commander Alexander Leslie came to Salem in search of cannons he believed were hidden there some of the locals taunted him, refusing to let his troops cross the bridge into town, and scuttled his boat. During the confrontation the Salem militia gathered, armed and ready for a fight. To save face, and his troops, he ordered his men to return to Boston. On their way out, Sarah Tarrant hurled insults at the retreating redcoats, one of whom stopped and aimed his musket at her despite Leslie's order to stand down. Fortunately, the soldier didn't fire, otherwise it's possible the Revolutionary War would have started then and there.

COLONIAL HOMOPHOPIA

In 1647, when Manhattan was still a Dutch Colony, a married barber-surgeon, (A common career at the time) named Harmen Meyndertsz van den Bogaert was caught sodomizing another man—a black slave. Sodomy was a capital offense according the strict Calvinist faith practiced by the Dutch at the time. Van den Bogaert was arrested but broke out of custody and fled with his lover to an Iroquois village, but was tracked down. In the ensuing struggle to capture him, a shoot-out occurred and a longhouse was set on fire. He was dragged away by the posse and returned to Fort Orange. He escaped a second time, but drowned in the attempt, possibly making him the first victim of homophobia in North America.

POPULAR VIRGINIA
In 1775, over two million people lived in the thirteen American colonies with about 25% of them residing in Virginia alone.

THE "REAL" FIRST POTUS
Some historians challenge the commonly held belief that George Washington was the first President of the United States. Some claim that it was really a man named John Hanson who died in 1783. Sometimes called the "Forgotten President", Hanson was the first elected "President" under the Articles of Confederation. The Articles of Confederation, which were formally known as the Articles of Confederation and Perpetual Union, were an agreement among all thirteen original states that served as the First Constitution. It's drafting by a committee appointed by the Second Continental Congress began on July 12, 1776, and an approved version was sent to the states for ratification in late 1777. The formal ratification by all thirteen states was completed in early 1781. Government under the Articles was superseded by a today's Constitution and Federal form of government in 1789.

EARLY HOUSING
When the colonists first landed in America they had to quickly find some kind of shelter. Their first homes were dugouts, then huts, and finally cabins. The walls of the dugouts were made out of tree branches woven together and plastered with mud.

COLONIAL PARENTING
Becoming a parent in Colonial America was both tough and risky. 10% of all infants died before the age of one. A full half of slave children died

before their first birthday, and 40% of children died before age 6. This was the case with all classes of people. Disease, disaster, weather and accidents all played large roles in the high death rates of Colonial children. Infant mortality rates were so high in the mid 18th Century in the future United States families typically did not name a child until he or she had reached the age of two: prior to that time, parents would call the baby "it," "the little angel," or "the little visitor."

THE FIRST "LEGAL" SLAVE OWNER IN AMERICA WAS ACTUALLY BLACK

Prior to 1655 there were no legal slaves in the colonies, only indentured servants. All masters were required to free their servants after their prede-termined time, or "indenture" was up. Seven years was the limit that an indentured servant could be held. Upon their release they were granted 50 acres of land. This included any Negro purchased from slave traders. Blacks were also granted 50 acres upon their release.

Anthony Johnson was a Black man from modern-day Angola. He was brought to the US to work on a tobacco farm in 1619.

When Anthony was released he was legally recognized as a "free Negro". In 1651 he owned 250 acres and five black indentured servants. In 1654, it was time for Anthony to release one by the name of John Casor. Casor worked for Johnson as an indentured servant. Instead Anthony told Casor he was extending his time. Casor left and became employed by the free white man Robert Parker.

Anthony Johnson sued Robert Parker in the Northampton Court in 1654. In 1655, the court ruled that Anthony Johnson could hold John Casor indefinitely. The Virginia court then gave judicial sanction for blacks to own slaves of their own race. Thus Casor became the first permanent slave and Johnson the first slave owner of a lifetime legal slave.

BEFORE NEW JERSEY

New Jersey was originally called Lorraine and New Sweden. New Sweden, the first Swedish colony in America, took in the Garden States southern most counties, parts of Delaware and Pennsylvania. Although details are few because the settlement only lasted about 17 years with a maximum population thought to be about 500.

BEFORE NEW YORK

New Amsterdam was a 17th-century Dutch settlement established at the southern end of Manhattan Island, which served as the seat of the colonial government in New Netherland. It became a provincial extension of the Dutch Republic as of 1624 and was designated the capital of the province in 1625.

New Amsterdam was renamed New York on September 8, 1664, in honor of the then Duke of York (Who later became James II, in whose name the English had captured it.) In 1667 the Dutch gave up their claim to the town and the rest of the colony, in exchange for control of the Spice Islands.

NEW YORK'S INDEPENDENCE DAY

When the Continental Congress declared independence from Britain the official vote was 12 Colonies in favor, 0 against. Yes that's right just 12 and not 13. The colony of New York abstained from the original vote on July 2. New York did not vote to join the fight for independence until July 19. Weeks after the Declaration of Independence had already been signed.

COLONIAL CURRENCY

Due to a chronic shortage of official English coin, colonists often bought and sold items with tobacco or other "rated commodities," to which colonial authorities assigned a certain value in pounds, shillings, and pence. In addition to using tobacco leaves for commerce, each colony printed its own paper money and also acted as a currency trader, assigning a value to foreign money, often Spanish dollars, and English pounds. Because the value of that paper money and foreign coin depended on each colony's proclamation, it was known as "proclamation money." This, for all intents worthless "money" inspired England to issue a "Commerce Clause" after England based Merchants complained of being paid with unreliable currency. Many historians believe it was the Commerce Clause, which forced

Colonists to trade with English merchants in English Pounds, that was the main provocation for the Revolutionary War

ILLEGAL CHRISTMAS

For 200 years Christmas was considered an Ancient Pagan Holiday. In 1647, under Oliver Cromwell the English Parliament banned Christmas. That ban was lifted after 12 years only for it to be reimposed in the Massachusetts Bay Colony in 1659. This ban on Christmas, becoming law in many places, lasted until the state of Alabama made Christmas a legal holiday in 1836. (The purpose of the law was to make Christmas day a bank holiday which was the first "official" recognition of the day) Meaning there was almost 200 years during which Christmas in the US was just another day. The US Government made it a federal holiday in 1870. (Oklahoma became the very last state to make Christmas a legal holiday again in 1907)

COLONIAL COURTSHIPS

In the 1700s, about one third of girls were pregnant when they married.

In the northern colonies, it was common for courting couples to engage in the tradition of "bundling" or "bed courting": spending the night in bed together, fully clothed. The point of this custom was to help establish whether or not they were compatible with one another.

Traditionally, participants were adolescents, with a boy staying at the residence of the girl. They were given separate blankets and expected to talk throughout the night. Occasionally a bundling board or bundling sack was placed between the boy and girl to discourage sexual conduct. Obviously with the high rate of premarital pregnancies the intended purpose of bundling, to determine compatibility, either failed or succeeded, at least 30% of the time depending on your point of view.

THE "BRIDE BRIGADES"

During the early 18th Century when the French controlled the Gulf of Mexico territory including Louisiana, they had a man problem; too many of them for the available ladies. These new settlers included soldiers, tradesmen and of course were valuable to the growing region but as all governments of the time understood, a successful colony requires families, not just single men. Obviously this meant the men needed wives.

However, finding ladies willing to marry a stranger and endure the rough frontier with their husbands wasn't easy. Beginning in 1704, the Compagnie des Indes (Company of the Indies) which held the monopoly on trade in the area sent 20 young French women between the ages of 14 and 18 to Louisiana via the ship Le Pélican. These "Pelican girls" as they became known, were snapped up by men desperate for marital bliss and of course the generous dowry subsidized by the King didn't hurt either.

Over the next few years other shipments of volunteer brides were sent. Many were orphans, some from "houses of correction". The most famous were the seventy-eight upstanding "casket girls" named after the small casket like suitcases that carried their belongings. Upon arrival, they were sent to a newly built convent in New Orleans until they found husbands. Today, claiming a "casket girl" as an ancestress is a matter of pride for native Louisianans.

IN GOD WE TRUST

There has been much debate over whether or not America was founded as a Christian Nation. While some of the founders were Christians and others Deists (Deists believe in the existence of a creator on the basis of reason but reject a supernatural deity who interacts with humankind.) It is known that the framers did in fact believe in God. Want proof? The very first resolution brought before the First Continental Congress, and immediately passed, was the declaration that they would open every meeting with a prayer. Which, if you think about it is kind of odd for the Deists considering prayer by it's very nature denotes an interactive relationship with God. Were the Deists just being considerate? Perhaps, or maybe they were just hedging their bets.

7

The Unknown Presidents

Stuff you just never learned in school

HartofAmerica.net

GEORGE WASHINGTON 1789-1797 gave the shortest inaugural speech in American history on March 4, 1793. It was only 133 words long. Of the founding fathers that did become President, only Washington did not attend college. George Washington never lived in the White House the capital was actually located in Philadelphia and other cities When Washington was president. He is the only president who didn't represent a political party.

* When George Washington found a lost dog during the battle of Germantown, he crossed enemy lines to return the wayward K9 to its rightful owner, General Howe, his opponent in the battle.

JOHN ADAMS 1797-1801 Adams defended British soldiers after the Boston Massacre. Although Adams objected to what he believed was unfair taxation by the British government, he also believed in the primacy of the rule of law. After the killing of five colonists in the March 1770 Boston Massacre, Adams volunteered to represent the nine British soldiers charged with manslaughter to ensure they received a fair trial. Adams argued that the soldiers fired in self-defense against "a motley rabble" and won a surprising acquittal for seven of the nine defendants.

* He was the first president to live in the White House. The President moved into the White House on November 1, 1800. Construction not quite completed and the home reeked of wet plaster and paint fumes.

THOMAS JEFFERSON 1801-1809 and John Adams both died on the exact same day, July 4th 1826. Jefferson felt that he would not last of the summer of 1826 but he hope to live through July 4th which was the officially recognized 50th anniversary of the Declaration of Independence. Jefferson wrote his own epitaph... On it it states the he was the author of the Declaration of Independence, the Statuette of Virginia for Religious Freedom and that he was the father of the University of Virginia, but made no mention that he had ever been President of the United States.

* Adam's last words were "Thomas Jefferson still survives" Not knowing that Jefferson had died earlier that day in Virginia.

* It is well known that Thomas Jefferson liked to party. He was known to throw frequent lavish parties spending up to $50 a day (About $980 in today's currency) on food and wine. Incidentally Jefferson died flat broke

JAMES MADISON 1809-1817 Madison was the shortest of all the Presidents at only 5'4". He never weighed more than 100 pounds.

* He once lost an election because he didn't give alcohol to voters. In 1777 a young James Madison lost a bid for election to the state's House of Delegates. He would later write that the defeat was the result of his refusal to provide free liquor to the voters on Election Day, a common custom then known as "swilling the planters with bumbo." The future president believed that bribing electors with booze was contrary to republican principles.

JAMES MONROE 1817-1825 Monroe died exactly to day 5 years after Thomas Jefferson and John Adams on July 4, 1831.

* The founding of Liberia in the early 1800s was motivated by the domestic politics of slavery and race in the United States as well as by U.S. foreign policy interests. In 1816, a group of white Americans founded the American Colonization Society (ACS) to deal with the "problem" of the growing number of free blacks in the United States by resettling them in Africa. The resulting state of Liberia would become the second (after Haiti) black republic in the world at that time. The Capital of the African Nation, Monrovia, is named after James Monroe who was a prominent supporter of the colony in sending freed Black slaves and ex-Caribbean slaves from the U.S. and Caribbean Islands to Liberia because he saw it as preferable to emancipation in America

JOHN QUINCY ADAMS 1825-1829 John Q. Adams, was the first President to be the son of a former President.

* Adams loved to skinny dip in Washington's Potomac River.

* Quincy Adams was the only former President to serve in the U.S. House of Representatives. In 1830, Adams was elected to the House as part of the Massachusetts delegation; he would represent three districts over the course of his Congressional Career. He was also the first House member to champion abolition and emancipation

ANDREW JACKSON 1829-1841 Jackson was involved in over 100 duels, most to defend the honor of his wife, Rachel. He had a bullet in his chest from an 1806 duel and another bullet in his arm from a barroom fight in 1813 with Missouri Senator Thomas Hart Benton.

* Jackson was also the first President to experience an assassination attempt. Richard Lawrence, a house painter carried two guns that day. Both misfired. An event experts says had a 1 in 125,000 times chance of occurring. After Lawrence's attempts failed, Jackson chased him with his walking stick.

MARTIN VAN BUREN 1837-1841 The term O.K. derives from President Martin Van Buren who was known as Old Kinderhook because he was raised in Kinderhook New York. OK clubs were created to support Van Buren's campaigns.

* He is also the first United States citizen to become President. All previous Presidents were born British subjects. When Van Buren wrote his biography after serving as president he didn't mention his wife of 12 years not even once.

WILLIAM HENRY HARRISON 1841 Harrison gave the longest inaugural address at 8,443 words on March 4, 1841 on cold and blustery day in Washington DC. Because of his exposure to the elements He developed a severe cold and died one month later of pneumonia. Harrison holds the dubious honor of being the United States shortest serving Commander in Chief.

JOHN TYLER 1841-1845 Tyler had more children than any other President. He had eight by his first wife had seven by his second. He was 70 years of age when his last child, Pearl, was born. He was also the first President to get married in office. His children from his first marriage did not approve of the second so none of them would attend.

* After the death of Harrison, John Tyler assumed the Oval Office although amid some confusion since a President had never died in office. Since the transference of Presidential Power in this situation had not been considered up to this time, Tyler served out his term without a Vice President. (This has only occurred 3 other times in US history)

JAMES K POLK 1845-1849 Polk was not expecting to be the Democratic nominee for president in 1844. Martin Van Buren wanted to be nominated for a second term as president – which if he have won would have made him only one of two Presidents in US history to serve non consecutive terms - but his stance against the annexation of Texas was unpopular with the Democratic Party. The delegates voted nine times before compromising on Polk as their pick for president.

* Polk is considered by many to be the best one-term president in American History. He was a strong leader during the Mexican War. He added a vast area to the United States from the Oregon Territory through Nevada and California. A rare Politician as well, Polk kept all of his campaign promises.
    -Americanhistory.com

ZACHARY TAYLOR 1849-1850 In 1848, Taylor was nominated to be President by the Whig Party without his knowledge or presence at the nominating convention. The Whigs sent him notification of the nomination without the postage being paid, the party expecting Taylor to pay for the letter that told him that he was the nominee. He refused to pay the postage and did not find out about the nomination for weeks after.

* Taylor died unexpectedly on July 8, 1850. Doctors believe the cause was cholera. More than a hundred and forty years later, after much speculation, Taylor's body was exhumed to establish that he had not been poisoned. The Cause was not determined but experts did rule out intentional poisoning.

-Americanhistory.com

MILLARD FILLMORE 1850-1853 Fillmore's first elected office was to the New York state legislature in 1828 on the Anti-Masonic ticket, which, as its name suggests, strongly opposed Freemasonry.

* Fillmore did not have a Vice President. Since the Constitution did not originally include a provision for replacing Vice Presidents, in the event they ascended to the Oval Office. The office has been vacant for a total of about 38 of years. Over a hundred years later, 1967 to be exact, the 25th Amendment was ratified which allows the president to appoint a VP with Congressional approval.

FRANKLIN PIERCE 1853-1857 Pierce was a known alcoholic. In fact, he was criticized during the campaign and his presidency for his drinking. During the election of 1852, the Whigs mocked Pierce as the "Hero of Many a Well-Fought Bottle."

* Pierce's wife was Jane Means Appleton. They had three sons, all of whom died by the age of twelve. Pierce was not nominated for a second term and spent the last years of his life caring for his grieving wife in Europe.

JAMES BUCHANAN 1857-1861 Buchanan was the only U.S. President that remained a bachelor his entire life. As President he was virtually inseparable from William R King a senator from the state of Alabama earning the pair of the nickname "Miss Nancy and Aunt Fancy" by Andrew Jackson. Aaron Brown referred to King as Buchanan's "wife" and "better half" — suggesting that their relationship was not as "closeted" as one might think.

Obviously this situation raised many questions, the first being about Buchanan's sexual preferences and whether or not he was in fact, gay.

Although much of the evidence is circumstantial, it is none the less, compelling. For instance: Buchanan never married and was a lifelong bachelor. For many years he lived with another man, U.S. Sen. William King, a Democrat from Alabama. According to some, the two men were inseparable.

According to historian James Loewen, Buchanan instructed relatives to burn his private letters after his death. Some surviving correspondence from the era indicates a romantic bond between Buchanan and King, according to Loewen.

After being appointed minister to France by John Tyler in 1844, King wrote to Buchanan, "I am selfish enough to hope you will not be able to procure an associate who will cause you to feel no regret at our separation."

In that same year in a letter to a friend, Buchanan wrote of King's absence, "I am now 'solitary and alone,' having no companion in the house with me. I have gone a wooing to several gentlemen, but have not succeeded with any one of them."

Despite the preponderance of "evidence" neither man ever publicly admitted to being in a romantic relationship. So has America had a homosexual President? If so it certainly wasn't out in the open, but it does seem quite likely.

* The lack of a spouse in the White House and for that matter Buchanan's life, caused Buchanan to employ the services of his Niece, Harriet Rebecca Lane Johnston to serve as First Lady, or "Hostess" of the United States.

* Buchanan's administration was so contentious that members of Congress often carried knives and small pistols into their Legislative chambers. But he was also caring at times. Buchanan quietly but consistently bought slaves in Washington DC and then set them free in Pennsylvania.

ABRAHAM LINCOLN 1861-1865 Abraham Lincoln is the only US president that was also a licensed bartender he was co-owner of Barry and Lincoln saloon in Springfield Illinois. Lincoln logs are named after Abraham Lincoln and the log cabin he was born in. John Lloyd Wright son of famous Architect Frank Lloyd Wright invented the popular toy building set.

* Lincoln also was the first President to ever be photographed at his inauguration. In the picture he is standing near his future assassin, John Wilkes Booth.

* Lincoln is enshrined in the Wrestling Hall of Fame. Young Abe was an accomplished wrestler. He lost only once in approximately 300 matches and Lincoln could smack talk too. According to Carl Sandburg's biography of Lincoln, he once once challenged an entire crowd of onlookers after a victory: "I'm the big buck of this lick. If any of you want to try it, come on and whet your horns." There were no takers.

* Lincoln is also the only President to receive a patent. He was the first to have a beard, at the request from a little girl named Gracie Bedell.

* And was the first President to have a child die while he was in office. Willie Lincoln was only 12 when he died from what the Doctors called "bilious fever" which was a medical diagnosis of the day often used for any fever that exhibited the symptom of nausea or vomiting.

ANDREW JOHNSON 1865-1869 Johnson, Lincoln's Vice President who took office after Abe's assassination, was the first President to be impeached, although not convicted. He was acquitted by one vote in the Senate. It would be another 131 years before another President, Bill Clinton, would be impeached. (Although like Johnson, not convicted or removed from office).

* Johnson's father, Jacob died when Johnson was just 3 years old. His mother remarried and later sent him and his brother out as indentured servants to a tailor named James Selby. The brothers ran away after two years. On

June 24, 1824, Selby advertised in a newspaper a reward of $10 for anyone who would return the brothers to him. However, they were never captured.

* At 22 he was elected the mayor of Greeneville, Tennessee. He served as mayor for four years. He was then elected to the Tennessee House of Representatives in 1835. He later became a Tennessee State Senator before being elected to the congress in 1843.

ULYSSES S GRANT 1869-1877 Grants real first name was Hiram. Hiram Ulysses Grant changed it because he didn't want to enter West Point with initials like H.U.G. When Congressman Thomas Hamer filed Grant's application to West Point, he thought Grant's first name was Ulysses and assumed the middle name would be Simpson, Grant's mother's maiden name. Hence Ulysses S.

* It was so cold at Grant's inauguration that the canaries that were supposed to sing at the inaugural ball all froze to death.

* Grant smoked at least 20 cigars a day. After a big victory against the Confederate Army, a nation of well-wishers sent him more than 10,000 cigars. Grant died of throat cancer. But he did manage to finish his memoir and restore his families lost fortune before his death. (Grant had lost the family fortune after an investment firm he lent his name, and reputation to, went belly up).

RUTHERFORD B. HAYES 1877-1881 Hayes banned alcohol and held Gospel sing-a-longs every night in the White House.

* Hayes also started the tradition of the Easter Egg Roll on the White House lawn, which has been run on the Monday after Easter since 1878.

* The American consul in Bangkok knew Rutherford's wife Lucy Hayes loved cats and arranged in 1878 for the delivery of the first Siamese cat in America. The cat arrived in 1879 and the Hayeses named it Siam.

JAMES GARFIELD 1881 James Garfield was the first president to ever talk on the phone when he spoke to Alexander Graham Bell who was on the other end of the line 13 miles away.

* Garfield was a brilliant man able to write in both Latin and Greek and he could do so with both hands.

* Garfield was assassinated by an anarchist named Charles Guiteau. Guiteau shot Garfield in the back with a five barrel .44 caliber pistol called a British bulldog and 1881. He said he chose a gun because it would look good on display in a museum someday. No one currently knows where the gun is. Garfield didn't die from the gunshot wounds. He died of blood poisoning after doctors tried to remove the bullet from his Back with their dirty fingers and instruments causing him to linger for 80 days before dying. Guiteau later claimed he didn't kill the president because the doctors had.

CHESTER A. ARTHUR 1881-1885 President Arthur made no Inaugural Address At the request of Arthur, the International Meridian Conference was held in Washington, D.C. in October 1884 to determine the Prime Meridian of the world. The conference established the Greenwich Meridian and international standardized time, which are both still recognized today.

* After Garfield's death, Arthur insisted the White House be redecorated and had twenty-four wagonloads of furniture hauled off and sold at public auction. The pieces included some dating back to John Adams' term and would be considered priceless today.

GROVER CLEVELAND 1885-1889 Cleveland was the only U.S. President to be elected to two non-contiguous terms.

* Cleveland's real first name was Stephen but he changed it to Grover as an adult.

* The Baby Ruth Candy Bar was named after his daughter Ruth and not Babe Ruth as some have speculated.

* Cleveland is the only present history to hold the job of a hangman. He was once a Sheriff of Erie county New York and twice had to spring the trap at a hanging.

BENJAMIN HARRISON 1889-1893 Benjamin Harrison was the grandson of President William Henry Harrison, the 9th President of the United States. Benjamin was seven years old when his grandfather was elected president.

* Benjamin Harrison defeated the incumbent President Grover Cleveland in the election of 1888. However, in his bid for re-election in 1892, Harrison was defeated by Cleveland making it the only time an incumbent president was defeated by a former President.

* The Election of 1892 also gave us another first. It was the first time no candidate campaigned in a presidential election. Neither Harrison nor Cleveland actively campaigned, relying on surrogates instead. Maybe an idea modern day candidates should consider?

GROVER CLEVELAND 1893-1897 (Again) During Cleveland's second term He Repealed the Sherman Silver Purchase Act and returned the US currency to a gold standard. The subsequent run on government gold required that the government borrow from the New York financier J. P. Morgan

WILLIAM MCKINLEY 1897-1901 McKinley's inauguration was the first presidential inauguration to be filmed.

* McKinley was the first President to ride in a self propelled vehicle. It was an electric ambulance that took him to the hospital after he had been shot

inside the Temple of Music on the grounds of the Pan-American Exposition in Buffalo, New York. McKinley was shaking hands with the public when he was shot by Leon Czolgosz.

* After Czolgosz shot McKinley, the crowd subdued him and began to beat him severely. The wounded McKinley shouted "Boys! Don't let them hurt him!"
    McKinley died eight days later

THEODORE ROOSEVELT 1901-1909 Teddy bears were so named when Theodore Roosevelt refused to shoot a small bear cub one day. The incident was reported in the news which inspired a toy manufacturer to come out with the stuffed animal.

* Contrary to popular belief Teddy Roosevelt and not John Kennedy was the youngest U.S. President. He was 42 when he became Chief Executive following the assassination of William McKinley. However in fairness to popular belief, Kennedy was the youngest "elected" President, capturing the office at 43

* Roosevelt was shot by a would be assassin during his second run for the Presidency while giving a speech in Milwaukee Wisconsin. He went on to finish the speech with the bullet still lodged in his chest. Saying to the audience:
    "I don't know whether you fully understand that I have just been shot,
    "I give you my word, I do not care a rap about being shot; not a rap."

WILLIAM HOWARD TAFT 1909-1913 Taft was a big boy. The largest President at 325 pounds he was dubbed "Big Bill" and often got stuck in the White house bath tub. His own advisers had to sometimes pull him from the tub.

* Taft is the only former President to serve on the Supreme Court. Though he's best remembered for his one-term stint, Taft became Chief Justice

in 1921, Once famously declaring "I don't remember that I was ever president."

*He debuted the Presidential pitch. It was Hall of Famer Walter Johnson that managed to snag a low-flying ball Taft lobbed from the stands at the start of a 1910 Washington Senators game. Over a century later, this opening day tradition is still going strong.

WOODROW WILSON 1913-1921 Wilson was the first President to show a movie in the White House: "The Birth of a Nation", which has become the most banned film in American History. What makes "Birth" most offensive is its depiction of its black characters performed by white actors in blackface — during Reconstruction. Made by D.W. Griffith. Birth of a Nation depicts defeated Southerners being terrorized by illiterate, corrupt and uncouth former slaves under the influence of white Northern carpetbaggers.

* Wilson was known to paint his golf balls black during the winter months so the avid golfer could continue play in the snow.

* The 1912 election wasn't a popular landslide. Wilson won easily in the Electoral College against the divided Taft and Roosevelt factions, but his 42% popular vote total was the third-lowest winning tally in history.

* Wilson is the only U.S. President buried in Washington, D.C. The 28th President is in a sarcophagus at the Washington National Cathedral. William Howard Taft and John F. Kennedy are at Arlington, Virginia.

WARREN G. HARDING 1921-1923 Genetic analysis has proved that President Warren G Harding fathered a child out of wedlock with long rumored mistress Nan Britton. Britton set off quite the scandal when she went public with her tale of the tryst in the White House boldly publishing her story 1927 best-selling memoir called "The Presidents Daughter'" But historians havw long questioned the Claim and Harding Defenders have vilified her as a liar for nearly 90 years. However based on DNA from Britton's grandson and descendants of Harding, the results are 99.9% accurate. The child born of their union, Elizabeth Ann Blaesing is the only known offspring of the 29th President.

CALVIN COOLIDGE 1923-1929 Calvin Coolidge was the only U.S. president to be sworn in by his own father

* Coolidge was a real prankster. On occasion he would press all the buttons on the Presidents desk and hide behind his door until his staff ran into the Oval Office. He would then pop out from behind the door and say that he was just trying to see if everyone was working.

* Coolidge was considered by many to be hyper shy and perhaps stand offish, even somewhat eccentric. He enjoyed riding a mechanical horse as much as he could while acting as if he was a cowboy. He often walked around with a raccoon that was perched behind his neck.

* But he was quite witty. His wit was described as 'sharp and cold as a frost-etching on a windowpane.' At a dinner party, the woman sitting next to him said she made a bet she could get more than two words out of him. Coolidge famously responded: "You lose."

As the story goes... President Coolidge and his wife Grace both visited a government farm on separate tours. The First Lady came to the chicken yard and showed some interest in a prize rooster. The farmer told her the rooster could mate several times a day. Mrs. Coolidge said, "Tell that to the president when he comes by." The farmer told the president. Coolidge asked, "Same hen every time?" The reply, "Oh, no, Mr. President, a different hen every time." Coolidge said, "Tell that to Mrs. Coolidge."

HERBERT HOOVER 1929-1933 He was the first president born west of the Mississippi River. He was a member of Stanford University's inaugural class. In 1891, Hoover enrolled in the new university. While he failed Stanford's entrance examination, the professor who administered the test admired his "remarkable keenness" and admitted him conditionally.

* Before Hoover became President, he starred in the first television broadcast in American history. While serving as secretary of commerce under Calvin Coolidge, Hoover's voice and image were transmitted live over telephone wires in the first American demonstration of television on April 7, 1927

* Hoover never held elective office until he won the 1928 presidential campaign. Before becoming the 31st president, Hoover had been appointed to his previous government positions.

FRANKLIN ROOSEVELT 1933-1945 Roosevelt was distantly related to both his wife and 11 other presidents.

* An only child with maternal roots dating back to the Mayflower, Roosevelt attended Harvard College, where he began courting another Roosevelt, Anna Eleanor, his fifth cousin once removed. When the couple married in 1905, Theodore Roosevelt took a break from his White House duties to give Eleanor away in lieu of her deceased father. Theodore was reported as saying to young FDR at the wedding, "Well, Franklin, there's nothing like keeping the name in the family." Though Theodore was his closest relative to head the country, FDR claimed to have traced his family tree to 10 other presidents as well.

* Roosevelt tried to increase the size of the Supreme Court.
    Fed up with the U.S. Supreme Court for striking down several New Deal laws, Roosevelt in early 1937 proposed expanding the court from nine to as many as 15 justices. Known as the Judicial Procedure Reform Bill, this so-called "court-packing" plan, was a plan critics claimed a separation of powers violation. Although FDR's fellow Democrats held large majorities in both houses of Congress, they balked at supporting his agenda.

In losing the battle, though, Roosevelt won the war. Never again would the Supreme Court invalidate a piece of New Deal legislation, and by the time of his death, seven of the nine justices were his appointees.

HARRY S TRUMAN 1945-1953 The letter "S" in Truman's full name does not stand for anything, as such it is grammatically correct to spell his full name without a period after it.

* Because the KKK was a powerful political force Truman was encouraged to join the organization. According to some accounts he was inducted though he was never active. Other accounts claim that he gave the KKK a $10 membership fee, but demanded it back. He was never initiated.

* Truman was a very accomplished pianist. As a child, woke at 5 a.m. every morning, practicing piano for two hours. At first, his mother taught him, but she eventually sent him to a more experienced teacher. At the age of 15, he abruptly quit his lessons, but he continued to play piano throughout his life.

DWIGHT DAVID EISENHOWER 1953-1961 His birth name was actually David Dwight Eisenhower. His parents originally gave him the same first name as his father—David. However, the future president's mother, Ida, soon had second thoughts. She didn't want her boy mistakenly called David Eisenhower Jr. or deal with the confusion of having two Davids in the house, so she transposed his name to Dwight David Eisenhower. His original birth name, however, remained inked in the family Bible and was printed in his high school yearbook.

* Eisenhower detested squirrels, at least around the White House. The reason: In the spring of 1954, the American Public Golf Association installed an outdoor putting green just steps away the Oval Office. To the dismay of Eisenhower, who was an avid golfer, the squirrels who roamed the White House grounds continually dug up the putting green to bury their acorns

and walnuts. Eisenhower was reported to have said to Secret Service agent John Moaney "The next time you see one of those squirrels go near my putting green, take a gun and shoot it. The Secret Service, however, wisely avoided the use of guns, and instead groundskeepers trapped the squirrels and released them into Rock Creek Park.

JOHN F. KENNEDY 1961-1963 During his time in office, both as a congressmen and later as President, JFK donated his entire salary to various charities.

* He and Jackie Kennedy actually had four children. In addition to Caroline and John, Jr., the Kennedy's had two other children. In 1956, Jackie gave birth to a stillborn girl whom the couple intended to name Arabella, and on August 7, 1963, Patrick Bouvier Kennedy was born five-and-a-half weeks early. The baby weighed under five pounds and died two days later from a pulmonary disease. The bodies of the two children were removed from Massachusetts in 1963 and buried next to their father in Arlington National Cemetery.

* Kennedy received last rites three times before serving as President. Kennedy suffered from poor health his entire life and, fearing imminent death, America's first Catholic president received the sacramental last rites of the church on three occasions. First during a trip to England in 1947, Kennedy fell ill and was given perhaps a year to live after being diagnosed with Addison's disease, a rare disorder of the adrenal glands. While returning to America aboard the Queen Mary, he was so ill that a priest was summoned to administer last rites again. He received the sacrament again in 1951 after suffering from an extremely high fever while traveling in Asia and a final time in 1954 after he slipped into a coma from an infection after surgery to address his chronic back problems.

LYNDON B. JOHNSON 1963-1969 Lyndon Johnson affectionately called the many women he slept with his "harem" He even had a buzzer system installed that rang inside the oval office so that the Secret Service could warn him what his wife was coming.

* Johnson won election to the U.S. Senate in 1948 after winning a Democratic primary by 87 of the 988,000 votes cast. During those years in Texas there was so few Republicans winning the Primary all but assured a victory in the General. Allegations of voter fraud on both sides are still debated to this day. The margin of victory for Johnson was so thin it became known as the Landslide Lyndon incident.

RICHARD M. NIXON 1969-1974 Lee Harvey Oswald may have actually planned to assassinate Nixon instead of JFK. In the early morning of November 22, 1963, Richard Nixon rode through Dallas to Love Field to fly home after attending a Pepsi-Cola board meeting. Nixon saw the preparations for the motorcade that hours later would carry John F. Kennedy, the man who defeated him for the presidency three years prior.

After Nixon landed in New York, he learned that Kennedy had been assassinated. In an odd twist to the story, the wife of Lee Harvey Oswald testified to the Warren Commission that in April 1963 Oswald read a local newspaper report, tucked a pistol in his belt, and told her, "Nixon is coming", "I want to go and have a look."

After locking him in a bathroom, Oswald's wife convinced him to turn over his gun. The account was puzzling, since Nixon was not in Dallas in April 1963. Is it possible Oswald had no idea Kennedy would be in town the same day and any politician of note would do and Nixon was originally his "Target of convenience" in 63? History will never know.

* Nixon was a Quaker. Nixon's mother, Hannah, was a devout Quaker who instilled the faith in her husband and children. After the failure of his father's lemon grove in 1922 Nixon's family moved to the nearby Quaker community of Whittier. As a boy, Nixon went to Quaker meetings four times on Sundays and played the piano at church services. He enrolled at

Whittier College, a Quaker institution, and attended mandatory chapel hours every day.

GERALD R. FORD 1974-1977 Gerald Ford was adopted. His birth name was Leslie Lynch King Jr.

* Ford was only person to serve as both Vice President and President without being elected to either office. The first person appointed to the vice presidency under the terms of the 25th Amendment, following the resignation of Vice President Spiro Agnew on October 10, 1973. Becoming president upon Richard Nixon's departure on August 9, 1974. Before being named VP, Ford served 13 terms in the House of Representatives.

* Ford could have played in the NFL. He won a scholarship to the University of Michigan, which he attended from 1931 to 1935. The university's football team, the Wolverines, won national championships in 1932 and 1933, and in 1934 (his senior year) Ford was named the team's most valuable player.

Upon graduation, Ford received offers from two professional football teams, the Detroit Lions and the Green Bay Packers, but he turned them down to take a position as head boxing coach and assistant football coach at Yale University, where he hoped to study law.

JIMMY CARTER 1977-1981 Jimmy Carter was the first president to be born in a hospital is also the first known President to go on record as having seen a UFO. Carter was the first Southerner elected to the Presidency following the Civil War. During his administration he pardoned and restored the U.S. Citizenship of Jefferson Davis who was the President of the Confederate States of America.

* Carter was a "dark horse" presidential candidate in 1976. The future President was tied for 12th in early polling, well behind former Alabama Governor

George Wallace and former nominee Hubert Humphrey. He used his image as a Washington outsider to defeat Gerald Ford in the general election.

RONALD REAGAN 1981-1989 Reagan won the "Most Nearly Perfect Male Figure" award from the University of California in 1940.

SECOND TIME IS THE CHARM

Ronald Reagan is the only US President to be elected after having been divorced. His first wife was Actress Jane Wyman who he married in 1940 and divorced in 1949, is best remembered as Angela Channing in the 1980s prime time soap opera Falcon Crest

* During the Hollywood Red Scare of the late 1940s and early 1950s, Reagan was active in film industry politics as chairman of the Screen Actors Guild (SAG).

He became an FBI informer in 1947, providing the Feds with the names of actors suspected of being Communist Party members or sympathisers. The names of the people that Reagan informed upon are redacted in his FBI file, but they were probably already known to the FBI from the testimony of former Communists, who were its main source of information about party membership in the film community.

* Because of his patriotism, FBI director J Edgar Hoover took a friendly interest in Reagan's political career. Shortly before Reagan announced his candidacy for the California governorship, the FBI discovered that his adopted son, Michael, had unknowingly become close friends with the son of Mafia boss, Joseph 'Joe Bananas' Bonnano. Hoover agents tipped-off Reagan so he could warn Michael to break off the association before it became an embarrassment and possible political baggage.

GEORGE W. BUSH 1989-1993 Bush is the first President to father a future President since John Adams.

* After the Japanese attack on Pearl Harbor in 1941, he enlisted in the Navy even though he had been accepted at Yale. Despite his father's disapproval, he signed up for the Navy's flight training program on his 18th birthday. When he received his pilot's wings, he was the Navy's youngest pilot.

* Bush played first base at Yale and was team captain. He played in two College World Series and had a career batting average of 251.

* After Ronald Reagan was shot by would be assassin John Hinckley, aides wanted Bush to chopper back to the White House but he refused, saying only the President lands on the South Lawn of the White House. He flew to the vice president's residence instead.

* Bush was the first sitting vice president to be elected president since Martin van Buren in 1836.

WILLIAM JEFFERSON CLINTON 1993-2001 Clinton was named after his biological father, William Jefferson Blythe, Jr, a traveling salesman who died three months before his birth. Clinton didn't assume his stepfather's surname until he turned fifteen.

* During his senior year in high school, he went to Washington, D.C. as a delegate in an American Legion civics program called Boys Nation. While on the trip, he met President John F. Kennedy.

* Clinton has won Grammies for "Prokofiev: Peter and the World", and "My Life", his autobiography.

* Although never an official Freemason. During his youth, Clinton was a member of the Order of DeMolay, a youth group affiliated with Freemasonry.

* There's a Bill Clinton Boulevard outside the US. Located in Pristina, Kosovo, the boulevard is named after Clinton for his help in the Kosovo War of 1998-99. A 10-foot tall statue of Clinton was added to the boulevard in 2009.

GEORGE W. BUSH 2001-2009 "W" was only the second President whose father also held the office. John Quincy Adams father, John, also held the office.

* Bush is one of only five Presidents to have won an election despite receiving less votes than his opponent. Al Gore received 543,816 votes more than Bush - but lost the electoral college 271 to 266, giving Bush the victory. As a result, Bush became only the fifth President ever to be elected having lost the popular vote - although he was only confirmed as President-Elect more than a month after the election due to the fact votes in Florida (where Bush won by just 527 votes) were originally scheduled for a recount before the US Supreme Court declared this move illegal.

* Bush was arrested for leading a crowd of "Yalies" in a post-match celebration which involved scaling the goalposts and trying to tear them down following a Yale-Princeton football game in 1967. Interestingly, however, Bush was also arrested at university a second time - less than six months previously. While drunkenly stumbling through the streets of New Haven, in December 1966, As the story goes Bush and his friends noticed a huge Christmas wreath on the front door of a shop. Bush and his friends tried to make off with the wreath, only for police officers to drive-by at that exact moment and catch them in the act - Bush would later admit he "might have had a few beers". Ya Think?

BARACK H. OBAMA 2009-2017 Obama was the first African-American president in US history, although his birth mother was actually caucasian.

* Obama's Presidency generated more conspiracy theories than any other President. Questions about his birthplace and thereby qualification to hold office plagued much of his Presidency. Other more bizarre allegations surfaced although none were ever proven. It is not known if the cause of these suspicions were based on his race or were more a matter of his time in history considering the ubiquitous use and popularity of the social media trend that allowed for widespread and unverified accusations.

* As a teenager, he experimented with drugs including marijuana and cocaine.

* Obama applied to appear in a black pin-up calendar while he was studying at Harvard but was rejected by the all-female committee.

* Obama won Best Spoken Word Album Grammy Awards for abridged audiobook versions of DREAMS FROM MY FATHER in February 2006 and for THE AUDACITY OF HOPE in February 2008. He beat Bill Clinton who was seeking his third Grammy with GIVING: HOW EACH OF US CAN CHANGE THE WORLD, a call to public service.

* Barack Obama owns a pair of boxing gloves one worn by Muhammad Ali.

DONALD J. TRUMP 2017 - _____

The election of the Forty-Fifth President of the United States, Donald Trump, the first "Non Politician" President in US history, caught many off guard. Although Trump lost the popular vote, he won with an Electoral Landslide.

As of this writing, it would be easy to claim that his adminitration rose to power during the most divisive period in American history since Abraham Lincoln. But we will leave that final judgement to history.

* Trump has never smoked cigarettes, drank alcohol or done drugs. His older brother, Fred, was an alcoholic for many years and warned Trump to avoid drinking. Fred ultimately died from his addiction.

* Trump's residence, Trump Tower, was used as the fictional Wayne Enterprises in "The Dark Knight Rises".

* Trump has actually run for president before. He won the California presidential primary for the Reform Party in 2000.

* The early days of his Presidency were marred by protests, anti-Trump Rally's and accusations of bigotry, mysogeny and aggressive policies.

We leave the final assessment of his – as of this writing – young administration, to future scrutiny.

8

Unknown Black History

The often ignored facts and faces that helped shape America

HartofAmerica.net

The retelling of history is often a funny and tricky task. Whether through time or negligence, stories are frequently embellished, misreported, attributed incorrectly, deemed unworthy of being told or their telling avoided altogether. While this phenomenon is not unique to any one ethnic group, it does seem to plague the Black race disproportionately considering the significance of these people, events and contributions when compared to the relatively small percentage of Blacks that make up the US population.

It is for this reason that UNKNOWN AMERICA is featuring the "Unknown Black History".

CHARLES DESLONDES

Ask people about the "slave rebellion" of the 19th century and most will mention Nat Turner. But Black Slave Overseer Charles Deslondes' attempt to seize the city of New Orleans in early 1811 is just as incredible a story of that of Nat Turner's. Deslondes planned his insurrection for years. He organized a force that stole uniforms and weapons from the local militias. It was a highly orchestrated attempt that was, like Turner's rebellion, eventually defeated by superior firepower and greater numbers. After his capture, Deslondes was brutally tortured and executed, and his followers massacred.

Some historians speculate the uprising was omitted from the history books because the idea of organized slaves with ideas about freedom and independence didn't fit the historical agenda.

HATTIE MCDANIEL

Best known for her role as Mammy in Gone With The Wind, McDaniel was the first African-American to win an Oscar. Though she got flak for playing "Uncle Tom" type roles, McDaniel fought for the rights of blacks to own homes and was active in community service. Ironically she was not allowed to attend the premier of "Wind" because she was black. She died in October of 1952 having broken yet another Black Barrier, though she was prohibited from publicly celebrating that victory.

THE WINDS OF ABOLITION

It was an American Colonial Court that legalized slavery in the 1600's in the new land and it was an American Colonial Court that helped pave the way for the end of it.

Mum Bett, a slave also known as Elizabeth Freemen, had the courage to face her master in a court case in Massachusetts in a case that would turn up the volume on the debate whether "Liberty and Justice for All", meant just that.

Sometime in the 1770s Freemen she was sold to Colonel John Ashley. Freeman was often abused by the colonel's wife, so she fled and refused to return. Freeman had often heard Ashley and his friends discuss the Declaration of Independence and the Bill of Rights, and she began to wonder why the statutes set forth in those documents should not apply to her. She enlisted the help of Ashley's friend, an attorney named Theodore Sedgwick.

In 1781, Sedgwick initiated the case Brom and Bett v. Ashley, in which he argued for Freeman's freedom using the Massachusetts Constitution, which stated that all individuals were born free and equal. The jury agreed with Ashley's argument, and the case set a precedent for the abolition of slavery in Massachusetts.

Bett was granted her freedom and 30 shillings in damages in 1781. And Mum Bett's case would be precedent ruling that would be debated and referenced for years to come.

CHARLES R. DREW

Drew was the first African-American to earn a Doctor of Medical Science degree. Drew heavily impacted the medical field of his time and today. Thanks to him, blood banks were created and he developed the way to process and store blood plasma. He led the blood banks of the United States and Great Britain but refused to do so after a law was passed calling for the segregation of the blood of African-Americans.

HARRIET E. WILSON

Before there was Ida B. Wells, Zora Hurston, or Alice Walker, there was Harriet Wilson. Wilson was the first African-American woman novelist.

In 1895 she became the first African-American to publish a book in the United States. Her book OUR NIG: SKETCHES FROM THE LIFE OF A FREE BLACK, detailed her life as an indentured servant and the physical and emotional abuse she endured. The book did not garner Wilson fame at the time it was written and was mostly lost to history.

Years later it was found by Henry Louise Gate, Jr., and confirmed as the first book published by an African American, by either sex, in America.

INOCULATION WAS INTRODUCED TO AMERICA BY A SLAVE

Few details are known about the birth of a slave named Onesimus, but it is assumed he was born in Africa in the late seventeenth century before eventually landing in Boston. Onesimus was a gift to the Puritan church minister Cotton Mather from his congregation in 1706.

While in Mather's possession, Onesimus told him about the centuries old tradition of inoculation practiced in Africa. By extracting material from an infected person and scratching it into the skin of an uninfected person, you could deliberately introduce smallpox to the healthy individual making them immune. Considered extremely dangerous at the time, Mather convinced Dr. Zabdiel Boylston to experiment with the procedure when a smallpox epidemic hit Boston in 1721. At least 240 people were inoculated using Onesimus' technique. Opposed for political, religious and medical reasons, public reaction to the experiment put Mather and Boylston's lives in danger despite records indicating that only 2% of inoculated patients died compared to 15% of people not inoculated against the disease.

Onesimus' traditional African practice was used to inoculate American soldiers during the Revolutionary War and introduced the concept of inoculation to the United States.

SLAVERY IN THE NEW WORLD

Of the roughly 12.5 million Africans shipped to the New World during the Transatlantic Slave Trade, fewer than 388,000 actually arrived in the United States.

In the late 15th century, the advancement of seafaring technologies created a new Atlantic region that would forever change the world. As ships began connecting West Africa with Europe and the Americas, native populations were decimated. The transatlantic slave trade began primarily due to the native labor force being so diminished. But with the growing need for plantation and mining labor, the transatlantic slave trade began to fill this void.

The Transatlantic Slave Trade was conducted from 1500-1866, shipping more than 12 million African slaves across the world. Over 400 years, the majority of slaves (4.9 million) found their way to Brazil where they suffered incredibly high mortality rates.

By the time the United States became involved in the slave trade, it had been under way for two hundred years. The majority of its 388,000 slaves arrived between 1700 and 1866, representing a much smaller percentage than most Americans realize.

Ironically it was a black man, Anthony Johnson, himself once a slave, that would be recognized as the nation's first "legal" slaveholder.

THE FIRST "LEGAL" AMERICAN SLAVE WAS OWNED BY A BLACK MAN

The slave owner was named Anthony Johnson. Johnson, a former slave himself, sued for the legal right, to hold indefinitely, another black man by the name of John Casor.

Here's how the story unfolds: In the mid 1600's John Casor was an indentured servant in Northampton County in the Virginia Colony. He was in service to Johnson, who was a free black.

In 1653 Casor filed what became known as a freedom suit claiming he had been imported for "seaven or eight yeares" as an indentured servant and that, after attempting to reclaim his indenture, he had been told by Johnson that he didn't have one. (Indenture)

According to the civil court documents, Casor demanded his freedom. Johnson's son in law, wife and his two sons persuaded Johnson to set Casor free."

Casor then went to work for an English Colonist named Robert Parker, who, along with his brother George, later testified that they knew Casor had an indenture.

In 1654 Johnson brought suit against Parker for detaining his "Negro servant, John Casor," saying "He never did see any [indenture] but that he had "ye Negro for his life". In the case of Johnson v. Parker, the court of Northampton County upheld Johnson's right to hold Casor as a slave, since there was no proof of the arrangement Casor claimed he had with Johnson.

In ordering Casor returned to his master for life, the court both declared Casor a slave and sustained the right of free blacks to own slaves. So in a legal sense, the first owner of a Black slave in the new America was in fact a Black man.

IMPROVISED INSPIRATION

Few people know that on a hot Wednesday in August of 1963 before a quarter million American's that Martin Luther King Jr. improvised the most iconic part of his "I Have a Dream Speech."

Standing on the top step at the Lincoln Memorial. Dr. King's remarks would conclude the Civil Rights March on Washington. As King stood at the podium, he pushed his notes aside. The original speech he had written just the night before was more political and less historic, according to Clarence B. Jones, and it did not include any reference to dreams. After delivering the now famous line, "we are not satisfied, and we will not be satisfied until justice rolls down like waters and righteousness like a mighty stream," Dr. King transformed his speech into a fiery sermon.

On stage near Dr. King, singer Mahalia Jackson reportedly kept saying, "Tell 'em about the dream, Martin," and while it is not known if he heard her, it could likely have been the inspiration he needed. Dr. King then continued, "Even though we face the difficulties of today and tomorrow, I still have a dream. It is a dream deeply rooted in the American dream...." And King preached on, adding repetition and outlining the specifics of his dream. And while this improvised speech was not considered a universal success at the time, today it is considered one of the greatest speeches in American history.

THE BLACK PATRIOTS

Contrary to much taught US Revolutionary War history, there were many Black Patriot fighters. One such man was Jack Sisson. Sisson was an African-American who served in the First Rhode Island Regiment. He was one of the key figures in the July 1777 capture of British General Richard Prescott. Sisson was among about forty troops under the command of Colonel William Barton. Barton and his troops, including Sisson navigated British controlled waters to sneak up and capture Prescott. Sisson served both as the pilot for one of the boats and also used his head to break down Prescott's door.

The capture of Prescott was a major embarrassment for the Brits and is thought to have reinvigorated waning US morale possibly causing a turning point in the war for US Independence. In part by Jack Sisson "using his head"

THE ORIGINAL FLAPPER

The iconic cartoon character Betty Boop is best known for her revealing dress, curvaceous figure, and signature vocals "Boop Oop A Doop!" While there has been controversy over the years, the inspiration for Betty has been traced to Black Jazz singer Esther Jones who was known as "Baby Esther" and performed regularly in Harlem New York's Cotton Club during the 1920s.

"Betty" was introduced in 1930 by cartoonist Max Fleischer. The caricature of the jazz age flapper was the first and most famous sex symbol in animation.

Baby Esther's trademark vocal style of using "boops" and other scat sounds caught the attention of actress Helen Kane during the 1920s. After seeing Baby Esther, Helen Kane adopted her style and began using "boops" in her songs as well.

Finding fame early on, Helen Kane often included this "baby style" into her music. When the character Betty Boop was first introduced, Kane sued Fleischer and Paramount Publix Corporation accusing them of using her image and style. However video evidence came to light of Baby Esther performing in a nightclub and the courts ruled against Helen Kane stating in fact, the "booping" style pre-dated her.

Baby Esther's "baby style" did little to bring her mainstream fame and she died in relative obscurity but a piece of her lives on in the iconic character Betty Boop.

THE FIRST BLACK SENATOR

Hiram R. Revels was born on September 27, 1827, in Fayetteville, North Carolina. Revels was a minister who, in 1870, was elected the first Negro United States senator by the state legislature (Which was how US Senators were elected at the time), representing the state of Mississippi. He served for a year before leaving to become the president of the historically black college, Alcorn Agricultural and Mechanical College

Debate surrounded Revels eligibility to serve based primarily on the 1857 Dred Scott decision, which excluded African-Americans from holding office. The decision was effectively reversed by the ratification of the 14th Amendment after the Civil War. Democrats had argued that Revels did not meet the nine-year citizenship requirement to hold congressional office given his ineligibility for citizenship during war years. But ultimately, Revels and his Republican allies prevailed arguing he was eligible based on his mixed-race background.

Revels election to Congress was particularly poignant in that the seat he was elected to had previously belonged to Jefferson Davis, the president of the Confederate States of America.

AN UNLIKELY AND "ILLEGAL" HERO

During the attack on Pearl Harbor on December 7th, 1942, African American Sailor Dorie Miller broke the rules to defend his nation and attempt to save US Servicemen lives. That fateful day Miller was working laundry detail when the Japanese Navy fighters attacked.

As Japanese fighters lay siege to the unsuspecting US Fleet, Miller sprung to action. First, he reportedly carried wounded sailors to safety, including his own captain. Then during the heat of the attack, Miller spotted an abandoned Browning .50 caliber anti-aircraft machine gun on deck and immediately decided to man the weapon. Though he had no training, Miller shot at the enemy aircraft until his gun ran out of ammunition, by some reports possibly downing as many as 6 Japanese Zeros.

What makes Dorie Millers story so incredible is that during this time in the US the Navy was segregated, so sailors of color like him weren't allowed to serve in combat positions. Instead, they worked as cooks, stewards, cabin boys, and mess attendants. They received no weapons training and were officially prohibited from firing guns.

Due to his heroic act, in March 1942, Rep. John Dingell, a Democrat from Michigan, introduced a bill authorizing the president to present Miller with the Congressional Medal of Honor. Sen. James Mead introduced a similar measure in the Senate. While Miller did not receive the Congressional Medal of Honor, he became the first African American Sailor to receive the Navy Cross.

Doris "Dorie" Miller died a hero almost two years later on November 24 while serving on the Liscome Bay when it was struck by a Japanese torpedo. Miller's parents learned of their sons death exactly two years later to the day, December 7th 1943.

Miller was posthumously awarded the Purple Heart, the Asiatic-Pacific Campaign Medal, the American Defense Service Medal, Fleet Clasp, and the World War II Victory Medal. There is also a frigate and a neighborhood on the US Navel Base in Pearl Harbor named in his honor.

9

The Unknown Framers

Some of the most misunderstood people in American history

HartofAmerica.net

The men credited with the idea that would become the America experiment were some of the most brilliant in history. Courage, vision and wisdom were common to most. Although their individual contributions to the new nation varied, most are regarded as true Statesmen.

Many of the Founders were actually younger than 40 years old in 1776. Several, such as Alexander Hamilton were in their twenties. Hamilton was just 21 when the Declaration of Independence was signed. (Hamilton himself did not sign the document) We tend to see them as much older than they actually were because of paintings that portrayed them later in life, most during their respective times while serving as Presidents or Supreme Court Justices. At the time of the Revolutionary War most were quite young. The cause of Liberty was actually a young man's and young woman's cause.

Some other youngsters at the time of the Declaration included:
(*Not all these were signers, but all played a role in the early establishment of the new nation.*)
James Monroe 18
Nathan Hale 21
Gouveneur Morris 24
Henry Knox 25
James Madison 25
John Jay 30
Thomas Jefferson 33
Samuel Chase 35
Ethan Allen 38
And John Hancock and Thomas Paine, both 39, round out the most familiar class of "Under Forty-Somethings."

The oldest Framers were:
John Hart 65
Stephen Hopkins 69
Benjamin Franklin 70
Samuel Whittemore 81

GEORGE WASHINGTON

Washington was born on February 11, 1731 under the Julian calendar. In the early 1750s Great Britain converted to the Gregorian calendar and so an adjustment was made and Washington's Birthday became February 22, 1732.

* Washington gave the shortest inauguration speech in American history on March 4 of 1793 It was only 133 words long. At the time of his inauguration, Washington owned the largest whiskey distillery in the country.

* Washington would bow at presidential receptions to avoid the physical contact of a handshake. This new "tradition" would last through the presidency of John Adams. Washington would rest one hand on the sword and the other holding a hat to avoid a remote possibility of anyone forcing a handshake. It was Thomas Jefferson that ended the tradition by shaking hands when greeting people.

* Washington's "wooden" teeth were partially made from real human teeth which he bought from his own slaves.

* When Washington died on December 14, 1799's last words were "I die hard but I'm not afraid to go let me go quietly I cannot last long it is well". He was so afraid of being buried alive, Washington asked in his will that he not be interred until three days after his death.

* The original intent was for George Washington to be buried beneath the rotunda floor under the dome of the capital but he died before the rotunda was finished in 1828 the crypt was covered up.

* He currently owes a little $300,000 in overdue library book fines

JOHN ADAMS

After graduating from Harvard University John Adams became a grammar school teacher. He was quoted as saying "I would rather sit in school and consider which of my pupils will turn out to be a hero and which a rake, which a philosopher and which a parasite than have an income of 1000 pounds a year.

* Adams was the only president to be father of a future president, John Quincy Adams, until George W. Bush became president in the year 2000 making Bush Senior the second president to have a son also become President.

* Adams was the first President to live in the White House when he came to Washington in DC in November 1800 however he was only there for four months after losing the election of 1800 to Thomas Jefferson. He also had a dog named Satan that lived in the Adam's White house.

* Adams died on July 4, 1820 at the age of 90 years 247 days he had the longest marriage of any ex-president. He and Abigail were married on October 25, 1764 and the marriage lasted 54 years

BENJAMIN FRANKLIN

Franklin was known as quite the prankster.

At just 16 years of age, Franklin regularly published editorials under the pseudonym Ms. Silence Dogood, a character he created. The writings of "Dogood" were so liked—a few eligible bachelors even mailed marriage proposals to the fictitious woman! Franklin actually often wrote with fake names. And many times did so while enjoying what he called "Air Baths". Yes ole Ben liked writing in the nude.

One of his most peculiar writings was an essay encouraging scholars to find a method for "improving the odor of human flatulence".

Throughout his life, Franklin was credited with authoring many hoax's. Because of this he was not allowed to pen the Declaration of Independence. It was feared he would slip a joke into the document. Which considering his history, was a valid concern.

* Franklin thought the Bald Eagle a bad choice for the new nations national symbol because it "was a bird of bad moral character that does not get his living honestly". Franklin felt the Turkey would be better because it was a "bird of courage, and "would not hesitate to attack a Grenadier of the British Guards." (It's historically interesting to note Franklin's concern over the morality of the Eagle... A common belief of most the Framers was work ethic was central to their definition of morality. When they spoke of "morality" they were not referring to anything having to do with promiscuity, but rather service and contribution to the good of the nation.)

* Franklin was the first to bring tofu to America.

* Franklin spent much of the war years in France wrangling for support from the French. While in France raising funds for the war, Franklin spent much of his time partying like a rock star, even while Mrs. Franklin lay ill back in the States. He also helped with negotiating the Treaty of Paris that ended the war.

* Benjamin Franklin died or April 17, 1790. While on his death bed his daughter asked him to change positions to improve his breathing and his last words were "a dying man can do nothing easy"

THOMAS JEFFERSON

At 83 years of age, Jefferson felt that he would not last of the summer of 1826 but he hope to live through July 4th which was the 50th anniversary of the Declaration of Independence. Ironically both he and John Adams died the same day on July 4, 1826 after long and distinguished careers they had earlier been friends and then political enemies and by the end of their lives stayed almost constantly in touch.

* Like Franklin, Jefferson was a "foodie" and is credited with bringing Macaroni and Cheese to the new Republic.

* John Adam's last words were "Thomas Jefferson still survives" Not knowing that Jefferson had died earlier that day in Virginia.

* Jefferson's last words were "Is it the fourth?" I resign my spirit to God, my daughter, and my country".

* Jefferson died flat broke. Before his death he was able to alleviate part of his financial problems by accepting $25,000 for his books from Congress. Those books were used to begin the Library of Congress.

Part of the reason for Jefferson's money woes was his extravagant lifestyle. He sometimes spend $50 a day (About $977 in today's dollars) for groceries and wine because of his lavish entertaining. Just the wine bill for the eight years he served as president was $11,000 (Almost $215,000 in today's economy)

* Jefferson's epitaph read: "Here was buried Thomas Jefferson author of the Declaration of Independence, of the Statue of Virginia for religious freedom, and the father of the University of Virginia however it did not include "President of United States"! (An achievement many of the early Presidents omitted in their respective lists of accompaniments)

JAMES MADISON
James Madison was known as the Father of the Constitution, since he was responsible for writing much of it.

* Madison was also responsible for proposing the resolution to create the various cabinet positions within the executive branch of government and 12 amendments to the constitution of which 10 became the bill of rights. Madison also proposed congressional pay would be determined by the average price of wheat during the previous six years of a congressional session. (Imagine tying Congressional compensation to economic prosperity today? What a novel idea!)

ALEXANDER HAMILTON

Hamilton founded the New York Post Newspaper. A paper famous for exposing, among other saucy news stories, the sexual exploits of US Politicians. Typically with provocative headlines. Oddly enough, Hamilton was the first American politician to have his career ruin by a sex scandal.

As the story goes… In 1791, Hamilton, a married man, met a young Philadelphia woman named Maria Reynolds, who claimed she needed cash because her husband had left her with a small daughter to support. Hamilton agreed to help, but their financial arrangement soon morphed into a trickier entanglement as the pair embarked on an affair that would last more than three years. But Maria Reynolds was no desperate housewife. She and her husband, James, had carefully planned the affair in an attempt to extort even larger amounts from then-Treasury Secretary Hamilton, who readily coughed up the sums.

Oh the juicy irony!

* Alexander Hamilton was killed by Aaron Burr in a duel in Weehawken New Jersey on July 4, 1804. Hamilton's son Philip had died in a duel three years earlier in 1801 at the exact same location. (The 4th of July has had many distinctions in American history)

JOHN HANCOCK

Hancock was a very brilliant man having graduated from Harvard at the age of 17.

* John Hancock may have been the richest man in New England after he inherited a shipping fortune after the death of his Uncle

* Some have accused Hancock of being a criminal, a smuggler actually. Goods like tea that arrived in New England on Hancock's ships may have avoided paying a duty. These suspicions led the British to seize Hancock's

ship, LIBERTY, which started a riot. John Adams got Hancock off the hook from the smuggling charges.

MYTH BUSTER ALERT!

Despite the lore it's not true that Hancock's over sized signature on the Declaration of Independence was done to taunt the King of England. The legend goes that Hancock stated that "King George will be able to read that!" In reality, Hancock was the first to sign in a matter fitting for the president of the Congress. All the paintings you have seen with the other "Signers" looking on is just another example of Revisionist History. There was actually only one other person even in the room at the time.

Hancock's signature was also printed, not signed. The signature was applied on the final copy of the document once the now iconic version was sent to the printer. It's fairly likely that the parchment Hancock signed on July 4th, 1776 was actually blank.

Some speculate part of the reason for signing a blank page might have been because his signature would have provided evidence of treason if things didn't go so well in the war!

SAMUEL ADAMS

Although commonly referred to as the "Father of America", Adams was a failure in business. From 1756 to 1764, Adams worked as a tax collector. As Tax rates mounted it became more difficult for the Colonists to pay up. As an advocate for the underprivileged coupled with his poor business acumen, Adams often simply looked the other way.

Although he would gain the affection of cash strapped taxpayers, he was in part responsible for the money issues the young republic faced. (Incidentally Adams became personally responsible for these debts, which of course he could not pay).

Adam's financial struggles were not limited to his professional life as a tax collector. He struggled to manage his own money as well. As such the "Father of America" often saw his family languish near poverty.

* Although Adam's was not near the top of the chain of command, he was often chosen to be the rebellious colonists spokesman. He was not a physically imposing man and he had a weak voice, but was said to move audiences by his sheer intellect and passion. Thomas Jefferson called him "Truly the man of the Revolution."

MYTH BUSTER ALERT!

* Despite popular lore, Sam Adam's did not brew beer. He did work for his fathers malt house which made malt that was then sold to breweries. Upon the death of his father, Adam's took control of the family business and from this point on would never be as successful as when his father ran the operation. The image on the line of modern day bottles of "Sam Adam's" beers, is also not that of Adams. Adams hair turned gray early, he was a sloppy dresser, and had dull washed out eyes. The Patriot that adorns the label of the popular brews is most likely that of another Patriot, Paul Revere.

* Adams is credited as saying, "It does not take a majority to prevail, but rather an irate, tireless minority, keen on setting brush fires of freedom in the minds of men."

THOMAS PAINE

Paine's Pamphlet, "Common Sense" remains one of the best selling books in American publishing history. In 1776 alone it sold over 100,000 copies. The writing laid the argument for American independence.

* When Thomas Jefferson drafted the Declaration of Independence, he drew heavily on Paine's work.

* He was also the first Patriot to use the phrase the "United States of America."

* Paine wrote the first volume of "The Age of Reason" while in prison in 1793 during the Reign of Terror. Paine was a devout atheist. He actually

critiqued the Bible from memory. Meaning despite the critique, he likely read the book in it's entirety. A feat few Christians can claim to have accomplished.

* While imprisoned in 1793, Paine narrowly escaped execution. In that day it was common for prison guards to chalk the doors of those who were condemned to die later that day. And the day came when it was Paine's turn. However since he was suffering from a fever the guards had agreed to keep his door open to allow fresh air into his cell. As a result the door was chalked but on the inside. When it was later closed, the guards on duty at that time missed the chalk cross that had been marked on Paine's cell door and so he narrowly escaped the guillotine.

* Only six people attended Thomas Paine's funeral in 1809. Due to his atheistic views and his condemnation of the Bible and organized religion, many former friends and colleagues had turned their backs on Thomas Paine.

In 1964 the Mayor of Thetford-in-Norfolk, Paine's hometown, said he would only approve a statue of Paine if it was stamped with the words, "Convicted Traitor". However the statue was eventually erected, sans the label and with Paine holding his book, "Rights of Man", upside down, supposedly to get people taking about the often very controversial works of this very controversial American Patriot.

PATRICK HENRY

Like Sam Adams, Patrick Henry was not the most astute businessman. He failed running a store for his father and after a period of time tried growing tobacco at which he also failed.

* In 1758 after three years of drought which resulted in low yield of tobacco crop, the Virginia assembly enacted the twopenny act, It fixed Anglican church minister salaries at two cents per pound of tobacco despite the market rate varying between four and six. A clergyman name James Maury sued Hanover county for damages. Henry defended the county against Maury's claims in a case that was to became known as the "Parsons Cause."

* Henry became known as a masterful orator. His he was effectively representing the American cause in the case of the Parsons Cause. He argued in favor of the twopenny act and compared the king of Britain who had vetoed the law, to a tyrant. He convinced the jury to grant the lowest possible award, one penny. The 1763 case developed Henry's reputation as a powerful and persuasive speaker. Parsons Cause is viewed as an important event leading to the American Revolution

* Patrick Henry is most famous for the speech he made in the house of Burgesses in March 1775. The House was undecided on whether or not to prepare for military action against the encroaching British army. Speaking in favor of mobilization. Henry ended his famous speech with the now and immortalized words, "I know not what course others may take but as for me give me liberty or give me death."

* Henry was instrumental in the adoption of the Bill of Rights of the Constitution. After the revolution he feared a strong national government was a threat to individual rights and that the president might become a king. He was a critic of the Constitution and was instrumental in having the Bill of Rights adopted to guarantee individual rights like freedom of religion, freedom of speech, freedom of the Press and more.

* Patrick Henry was married twice, first in 1754 he married Sarah Shelton and she bore him six children unfortunately she became ill and died in 1775. He remarried again at the age of 41 to 22-year-old Dorothea Dandridge. The couple had 11 children for a total of 17.

GOUVERNEUR MORRIS
Morris was an accomplished statesman that ushered in the idea of a person being a citizen of the union, not the individual states. As a delegate to the

Constitutional Convention in 1787, he played a leading role, speaking more often than any other delegate and contributing substantially to the writing of the U.S. Constitution.

* He was also a fierce critic of Thomas Jefferson. He was sharply critical of the foreign policy pursued by both Jefferson and James Madison, particularly their alleged hostility to Great Britain. Believing the War of 1812 to be "unjust, unwise, and mismanaged".

10

Unknown Religion

From the subliminal to the sublime. A peek
inside worship in the United States

THE FIRST "LEGAL" CHRISTMAS

The state of Alabama was the first state to recognize Christmas as a legal holiday in 1836.

So how did this occur? Puritans in the English Parliament eliminated Christmas as a national holiday in 1647, amid widespread anti-Christmas sentiment and accusations the celebration was more pagan than Christian (And considering the days raucous nature – it was mostly a party day – that belief was not entirely without merit).

But early settlers in New England went even further, outlawing Christmas celebrations entirely 12 years later in 1659. Well into the mid 1800's American's had different views on the date and meaning even between the North and South. Northerners even believing the date was sinful and that Thanksgiving celebrations more appropriate. But the move by Alabama wasn't so much Christian inspired as it was pragmatic. It was more to give "Locals" the day off to celebrate the day as they wished by creating a banking holiday. A date when commerce would be suspended.

After the Civil War ended, the traditions held mainly in the deep South at the time, began to spread Westward and finally across the newly reunited nation when in 1870 Christmas was declared an official US holiday by President Ulysses Grant on June 26, 1870. (Though not all states recognized the new holiday by this date).

(50 States.com)

SUBLIMINAL SALVATION

Charles Schultz's, A Charlie Brown Christmas, is a holiday classic spanning 5 decades. But did you know it contained subtle, yet very significant symbolism?

Symbolism that went unnoticed by most for many, many years!

During the scene where the "Gang" is practicing for the Christmas play Charlie Brown asks "Isn't their anyone who knows what Christmas is all about"? At this point Linus responds with: "Sure Charlie Brown I can tell you what Christmas is all about" and then he goes on to recite a verse from the Bible, Luke 2:8-14, which reads;

8 And there were in the same country shepherds abiding in the field, keeping watch over their flock by night. 9 And, lo, the angel of the Lord came upon them, and the glory of the Lord shone round about them: and they were so afraid. 10 And the angel of the Lord said unto them, *Fear not*: (Italics added) for, behold, I bring you good tidings of great joy, which shall be to all people. 11 For unto you is born this day in the city of David a Savior, which is Christ the Lord. 12 And this shall be a sign unto you; Ye shall find the babe wrapped in swaddling clothes, lying in a manger. 13 And suddenly there was with the angel a multitude of the heavenly host praising God, and saying,

14 Glory to God in the highest, and on earth peace, good will toward men. (KJV)

At the exact point where Linus says, *fear not*, he drops his security blanket which he is rarely seen not holding throughout the decades long cartoon series. It is thought by many that Schultz was reminding us of a clear message from the Gospels; that when we fear not, and put our trust in the Lord Jesus Christ, we can shed whatever "security blanket" we cling to.

Another poignant scene is at the conclusion of the program when Linus "Comforts" the spindly and wilting tree that Charlie had bought by wrapping his blanket around the tree's base as he proclaims "I never thought it was a bad little tree maybe it just needs a little bit of love" and the tree stands strong and upright.

Was Schultz trying to slide one by? Probably not, the message seems quite clear!

MANDATORY TITHING

During the colonial period in the US laws mandated that everyone attend a house of worship and pay taxes that funded the salaries of ministers. Eight of the original thirteen colonies had official, or "established," churches, and in those colonies dissenters who sought to practice a different version of Christianity or a non-Christian faith were sometimes persecuted.

BAPTISM FOR THE DEAD

Known as vicarious baptism or proxy baptism, the practice of baptising a living person on behalf of an individual who is dead, has been practiced since 1840 in The Church of Jesus Christ of Latter-day Saints where it is also called temple baptism because it is performed only in dedicated temples.

In the practice a living person, acting as proxy, is baptized by immersion on behalf of a deceased person of the same gender. The baptism ritual is as follows: after calling the living proxy by name, the person performing the baptism says, "Having been commissioned of Jesus Christ, I baptize you for and in behalf of [full name of deceased person], who is dead, in the name of the Father, and of the Son, and of the Holy Ghost. Amen."

The proxy is then immersed briefly in the water. Baptism for the dead is a distinctive ordinance of the church and is based on the belief that baptism is a required ordinance for entry into the Kingdom of God.

A CHRISTIAN PRINCESS?

Snow White and the Seven Dwarfs was the first animated movie made by Disney. And it is the only Disney movie to feature an openly Christian princess. Halfway through the film there's a scene where Snow White is shown praying. With head bowed and hands clasped together, she asks God to bless the seven little men who have been so kind to her. It's a short, but nonetheless poignant display of faith that is absent from most modern day features.

CYBER WITNESSING

In a typical week, about 20% of Americans share their faith online.

About the same percentage tune in to religious talk radio, watch religious TV programs or listen to Christian rock music.

POLITICS IN RELIGION

How often Americans attend church remains a strong predictor of how people will vote in elections. In the 2014 midterm elections, exit polls showed that those who attend worship services at least once a week voted for Republicans over Democrats for the House of Representatives by a 58%-to-40% margin. Meanwhile, those who never attend services leaned heavily toward Democrats (62% vs. 36%).

SEPARATION OF CHURCH AND STATE, NOT!

One of, if not the most misunderstood myths of the US Constitution is the belief by many that the phrase "Separation of church and state" appears in the Constitution. Although I would hope the majority of people reading this would understand the true history behind the phrase, far to many do not, and even worse, far too many that do, exploit this ignorance. The phrase "wall of separation between the church and the state" was originally coined by Thomas Jefferson in a letter to the Danbury Baptists on January 1, 1802. His purpose in this letter was to assuage the fears of the Danbury, Connecticut Baptists, and so he told them that this wall had been erected to protect them. The metaphor was used exclusively to keep the state out of the church's business, not to keep the church out of the state's business. To make the issue even more clear, Jefferson was not even referring to the US Constitution but that of the state of Connecticut.

The US Constitution states, "Congress shall make no law respecting an *establishment* of religion, or prohibiting the free exercise thereof." Both the free exercise clause and the establishment clause place restrictions on the government prohibiting any law to would interfere with religion. No restrictions are placed on religions except perhaps that a religious denomination cannot become the state sanctioned religion like the Founders were faced with in England where the Anglican Church was the official faith of the state

...BUT IN THE COLONIES? WELL YES!

Eight of the original thirteen colonies had official, or "established," churches, and in those colonies dissenters who sought to practice or proselytize a different version of Christianity or a non-Christian faith were sometimes persecuted.

THE NOT SO PURE PURITANS

The settlers of New England, credited with the first Thanksgiving, (Although this claim has been disputed) are most often portrayed as pious, strict, and rather devoid of any pleasures, especially of the flesh.

But the image of the pristine almost sinless Puritan, those first to arrive from Europe, is actually false.

According to Mary Beth Norton, a professor of American history at Cornell University, "The Puritans were typical people of their time in that they enjoyed the pleasures of the 17th century". They liked to drink. They liked to sit and talk. They liked to eat well and they enjoyed sex. They also liked to play games, like an early version of shuffleboard.

Pilgrims and Puritans alike promoted sex as a gift and duty from God, but only within the confines of marriage. One peculiar practice was that of having young couples that were courting actually sleep together before marriage to "get to know each other" Of course the purpose was not for sex but to test compatibility. However close proximity often gave way to other "ideas" and frequently lead to pregnant brides.

But the bottom line is, as history would like to paint the Puritans as pure, in the end they were just like most people, that is, human.

NO OATH FOR OFFICE

The No Religious Test Clause of the US Constitution is a clause within Article VI, that states no federal office holder or employee can be required to adhere to or accept any particular religion as a prerequisite to holding a federal office or a Federal Government job. This clause contains the only explicit reference to religion in the original seven articles of the U.S. Constitution. Of course the word "religion" also appears in the first Amendment.

Although hotly debated as to why the Framers added this to the original document, the true purpose of the religious test clause, dates back to the Corporation Act of 1661. This was the first of three Test Acts which were implemented in England. Under these acts, no one could hold office in England unless he swore an oath of fealty to the doctrines of the Church of England rather than God. This was the kind of religious test which the founders sought to avoid. They did not object to biblical qualifications. What they objected to was the requirement that all government officials be forced to swear allegiance to the codified doctrines of an established state church.

Unknown Politics

Weird stuff you probably didn't know, you didn't know

VOTE HERE

HartofAmerica.net

Michael P. Hart

A DIFFERENT KIND OF COLLEGE

Until the most recent US Presidential election, most Americans did not realize that Presidents must undergo two different votes to gain the Oval Office. One of course the popular vote where American Citizens cast their vote, and the second, the vote of the Electoral College which has the final say and does not occur until mid December when the electors meet in their respective state capitals.

What actually occurs on the first Tuesday after the first Monday in November, is a vote to determine how the electoral votes will be distributed. This system has lead to much debate and sometimes harsh criticism, but was intended by the Framers to keep the large population centers from exclusively selecting the President. When the electors meet they do not vote for a ticket but two ballots are cast, one for President and one for the Vice President.

Some states are "winner-take-all" based on the popular vote count of that state and some choose to divide their votes based on popular vote percentages for each candidate. Each state is granted one vote of each of its Congressional districts plus two more for its Senators.

It's is for this reason that the United States is not a "Democracy" in the purest sense but rather a Representative Republic. The electors representing the majority of voters wishes in their respective states. At least in theory. (Many have called for an abandonment of this system but to date no suitable or workable alternative has been presented)

THE "ABOVE GROUND" RAILROAD

Although President James Buchanan believed that slavery was protected by the Constitution, and he looked down on some of the actions that abolitionists took; thatwere usually in the form of open protest and strong oratory, Buchanan, the 15th President, would personally purchase slaves in order to free them to his home state of Pennsylvania.

-Whitegouse.gov

NO SECOND IN COMMAND

Millard Fillmore, John Tyler, Andrew Johnson and Chester Arthur, had no second-in-command for the entirety of their terms. Each began as Vice

President and ascended to the Presidency due to the death of the sitting President and since at this time in US history there was no Constitutional provision for filling the newly vacated office of the VP, this post remained vacant during their respective terms in office.

UNELECTED POTUS
John Tyler (1841-1845), Millard Fillmore (1850-1853), Andrew Johnson (1865-1869), Chester A. Arthur (1881-1885) and now Gerald Ford (1974-1977). All share another unique distinction. None were elected to office. They either ascended to office by way of their predecessors assassination, death from illness or as in the case of Gerald Ford... Richard Nixon.

WALLACE AND "THE DUKE"
In September 1968 while Alabama Governor George Wallace was running for President as a third party candidate on the Segregationist American Party, he began scrambling to find a running mate. His first choice was FBI Director J Edgar Hoover who declined. His next choice was John Wayne. Yep none other than the "Duke" himself. Wayne also declined informing Wallace he "was a Nixon man". However Wayne did like Wallace's position presumably telling Wallace during a phone conversation "You and I think the same way about what's happening to this country". The Duke would go on to send Wallace campaign contributions where on one of the checks memo lines he inscribed, "Sock it to 'em George".

DID YOU KNOW...
The Leader of the US House of Representatives, Known as the "Speaker of the House", does not have to be an elected member. Representatives are free to choose whomever they wish to lead the lower house. Although this has never occurred in US history it is in fact, legal.

A BIT OF ASSASSINATION IRONY
On April 14, 1865, Abraham Lincoln signed legislation creating the U.S. Secret Service. In perhaps an odd twist of irony, Lincoln would be assassinated later that same evening, at Ford's Theatre.

However even if the Secret Service had been established earlier, it wouldn't have prevented Lincolns death. The original mission of the agency was to combat widespread currency counterfeiting. It was not until 1901, after the killing of two other presidents, that the Secret Service established a security detachment assigned to protect the commander-in-chief as well as other dignitaries.

THE FIRST FEMALE "PRESIDENT"

Edith Bolling Galt Wilson was second wife of the 28th President, Woodrow Wilson. She served as First Lady from 1915 to 1921. After the President suffered a severe stroke, the First Lady took the Presidential reigns.

At end of World War 1, President Wilson traveled to Europe to negotiate and sign the Versailles Treaty and present his vision of a League of Nations, predecessor to the United Nations. Shortly after returning to the US he suffered a massive stroke and it was apparent to Mrs Wilson that he would not be able to fully function as the nations leader.

Her first move in establishing what she called her "stewardship" was to mislead the entire nation. Vetting the carefully crafted medical bulletins that were publicly released, The First Lady hid the truth of her husbands condition. When Cabinet members came to confer with the President, they got no further than the First Lady. If they had policy papers or pending decisions for him to review, edit or approve, she would first look over the material herself.

If she deemed the matter pressing enough, she took the paperwork into her husband's room where she would read all the necessary documents to him.

Mrs. Wilson "served" as the defacto President from October of 1919 until March of 1921. Until her death in 1961, the former First Lady insisted that she never assumed the full power of the presidency, at best she used some of its prerogatives on behalf of her husband. But some historians dispute this claim, insisting Woodrow was is such bad condition that Edith was in fact running the show, or in this case, the country.

-Whitehouse.gov – Biography.com

THE FIRST FEMALE SENATOR

Rebecca Felton was the United States first female Senator. Born in Decatur, Georgia, Rebecca was an invaluable asset to her husband's political career in the House of Representatives. A sharp and efficient woman, she deftly ran his campaigns and helped him write speeches and draft legislation. She was a passionate advocated for women's suffrage, equal pay, prison reform, and educational opportunities for the poor.

In 1922, when Senator Thomas Watson died suddenly, Georgia Governor Thomas Hardwick appointed 87-year-old Felton as a stand-in pending a special election. Thought to be a non threat to the Governor who was seeking the office himself, she was appointed with no intention of being sworn in when the Senate reconvened. However the Governor lost to Walter George.

As a slap in the face to the vanquished Governor, Felton was allowed to be sworn in by George with the understanding she would step down immediately. On November 21st Rebecca Felton was sworn in as the first female Senator, her Senate "career" lasting only 24 hours. She stepped down the following day when George was officially sworn in, but the end result of these political shenanigans is Rebecca Felton is officially the first woman senator in the U.S. and is still the only woman to have ever served as a senator from Georgia.

She also holds the distinction of having the shortest political career at the Federal level in US history.

EDWARD M. HOUSE - THE KING MAKER

House is a very curious figure is U.S. Political History. Known as "Colonial House" (A courtesy title since House had no military experience) During the early 20th century House played an important role as a campaign strategist and intra-party peacemaker and deserves part of the credit for getting Woodrow Wilson the Presidential nomination and then the presidency. Although the principal person responsible for Wilson's election was Theodore Roosevelt. Roosevelt's insatiable appetite for power led him to bolt the Republican Party and run as a Progressive Party (Bull Moose) candidate, thereby splitting the opposition vote with the popular sitting President Howard Taft all but ensuring a Democratic victory.

It is thought by many historians that Colonial House's primary role pre-election was to help get Wilson elected since he would be more receptive than Taft to the idea of a Centralized Bank, which Taft opposed.

Wilson's victory did in fact pave the way for the creation of the Federal Reserve Act, allowing for the creation of the Federal Reserve Bank, which is mostly privately owned and controlled, some claim by then associates of House and foreign interests favorable to House's "friends".

Many historians believe this was actually the chief reason behind the desire to get Wilson elected. After Wilson's victory, House played a more important role. Some believed House so powerful that he hand selected the majority of Wilson's cabinet members. Several Wilson hadn't even met prior to their appointment because the president-elect had little interest in the nuts and bolts of politics.

Prior to Wilson's election, House penned a book called Philip Dru, Administrator that pretty much detailed the forthcoming plan to "seize" the office and govern vicariously through Wilson. Although House telegraphed his strategy in the pages of "Dru", apparently no one picked up on the published plan. His agenda hiding in plain site.

THE PIONEERS OF WOMAN'S SUFFRAGE

The framers of the U.S. Constitution left it up to the individual states to determine their own voter qualifications. Some states imposed religious requirements on their citizens (although this pretty much ended by 1790). Others decided who had the right to vote based on property ownership. And then there was New Jersey.

The men who drew up the state of New Jersey's Constitution didn't have a problem with women voters provided they met the rather low property ownership requirement. When every other new state deliberately kept women from voting, New Jersey legislators embraced the radical idea that not only ladies should be members of the political community, but free blacks and aliens (non citizens), too.

This led to an unusual circumstance. According to the laws of the time, when a woman married, all her property became her husband's. Since a married woman owned nothing of her own in a legal sense, wives couldn't vote as they no longer met the property ownership requirement. However, no such bar existed for single women and widows.

Although women did not vote in great numbers, its seems the Garden State did in fact embrace woman's suffrage much earlier than the remaining states that were compelled by the 19th Amendment

TAG! YOU'RE THE POTUS

Known as the designated survivor - one person in the Presidential line of succession, is always kept at a secure, and undisclosed location when the President and the country's other top leaders are gathered at a single location, such as during State of the Union Address and Presidential Inaugurations. This is intended to guarantee continuation of government in the event of a catastrophic occurrence that kills the President and others in the presidential line of succession. If such an event occurred, the surviving official would become the acting President of the U.S. under the Presidential Succession Act.

Conclusion

As you can tell there is an enormous amount of misinformation, false reporting and just plain myths in the telling and teaching of the history of America.

With unfortunate frequency, this misinformation often ends up in our history books and worse, those text books used to educate America's youth.

This failure to accurately present the facts of American History often results in gross misunderstandings and false assumptions in today's America, especially when it comes to news reporting.

Not that the news media is reporting falsehoods but rather that the news of the day is better understood when you know the truth of the past of this great, but often misunderstood nation. And that a better understanding of the past affords everyone a better understanding of the world around us.

Instinctively people draw conclusions and make decisions based upon the most readily available information. When this information is incorrect, embellished or revised, it creates a false narrative that allows people to draw conclusions that are not accurate.

While portions of this book presents merely tidbits and trivia about life in America, much of it reveals the political, societal, and historical revisions that often cause people to make assumptions about the United States of America that are patently wrong.

It is the intent of UNKNOWN AMERICA to not only right some of the historical wrongs in the telling of the American story but also to hopefully inspire you to do your own research and to never take as gospel what you are taught, what you are told or what the Media offers as fact.

The United States of America is a fascinating country with a rich tapestry of history, people, events and oddities possessing almost endless stories and people to discover. Hopefully your journey of learning will continue far beyond the pages of this book and will be as enthralling, informative and entertaining as mine as I wrote this book, and by no means will my journey of discovery end with just this volume... And hopefully yours will not as well!

Go discover more of the UNKNOWN AMERICA for yourself, because...
"...there's a lot of history in the past"
Happy Discovering!
-MH

Resources

Whitehouse.gov
History.com
Biography.com
Movoto.com
The History Channel
The Bible (KJV)
Shadows of Power by James Perloff
Smithsonian.org
Military.com
New York Times
BBC.com
Congressional Research Service
50States.com
Businessinsider.com
mentalfloss.com
The Federalist Papers by James Madison, Alexander Hamilton and John Jay
The Washington Post
Mayflowerhistory.com
Jewish Virtual Library
Roadside America
Huffington Post
Biographyonline.com
Liveaction.org
Wikipedia.com
Foxnews.com
PBS.org
Holocaust Memorial Museum
livescience.com
techtimes.com
ozy.com

Michael P. Hart

The Library of Congress
The United States Constitution
The 5000 Year Leap by Cleon Skousen
The John Wayne Museum
The Bleacher Report
USA Today
Numerous personal interviews with various topic specific experts

About the Author

Michael Hart is a speaker, writer, consultant, political commentator and host of the Conservative talk radio program, The Michael Hart Show.

He is a frequent guest on radio and TV programs across the country and is a guest contributor to a number of publications

He speaks frequently on issues related to politics, culture, religion, business and personal growth.

Michael's ideas have been in featured in numerous publications including:

Forbes
Entrepreneur
Parade Magazine
Creative Selling
Sales and Marketing Executive Report
The Washington Post and numerous magazines, business journals, trade magazines and newspapers

He is the Director of Hart of America Productions based in Birmingham, Alabama. For speaking engagements and media appearances contact:

Hart of America Productions
5432 Villa Trace
Birmingham, AL 35244
205.362.6419
michael@HartofAmerica.net
www.MichaelHartShow.com

Other books by Michael

Mastering the Uncommon, Common Sense
"It really is the little things"